Safety advice
for bulk chlorine installations

HSG28(rev)

HSE BOOKS

© *Crown copyright 1999*
Applications for reproduction should be made in writing to: Copyright Unit, Her Majesty's Stationery Office, St Clements House, 2-16 Colegate, Norwich NR3 1BQ

First published 1987
Second edition 1999

ISBN 0 7176 1645 2

All rights reserved. No part of this publication may be reproduced, stored in a retrieval system, or transmitted in any form or by any means (electronic, mechanical, photocopying, recording or otherwise) without the prior written permission of the copyright owner.

This guidance is issued by the Health and Safety Executive (HSE). Following the guidance is not compulsory and you are free to take other action. But if you do follow the guidance you will normally be doing enough to comply with the law. HSE Inspectors seek to secure compliance with the law and may refer to this guidance as illustrating good practice.

Contents

Foreword vii

Introduction 1

Management of health and safety and risk assessment 3
Risk assessment 5

Design and location of installations 7
Potential incidents 7
Siting of installations 8
Unloading area 10
    Design and location 10
    Deliveries of liquid chlorine by road tanker or ISO tank container 12
    Interlocks 13
    Deliveries of liquid chlorine by rail tanker 14
Connections between the tanker and the fixed lines to the storage installation 14
    Types of connection 15
    Flexible couplings (semi-rigid loading arms) 15
    Flexible hoses 16
    Articulated arms 16
Pipework for liquid chlorine 17
    Permanent pipework at the unloading point 17
    Design criteria for pipework transferring liquid chlorine to storage tanks or
        from storage to point of use 17
    Protection of pipework 19
    Marking 20
Protection of liquid chlorine pipework against overpressure 20
    Provision of relief systems 20
Valves 22
    Types of valve 22
    Vertical globe valves 23
    Conical plug valves (PTFE-sleeved) 23
    Ball valves 24
    Remotely controlled valves 24
Storage vessels 24
    Design criteria 26
    Connecting pipework and means for isolation of storage tanks 27
    Liquid chlorine inlet 28
    Liquid chlorine outlet 28

Vent and compressed dry gas lines 30
   Relief system 30
   Instrumentation and chlorine detector systems 30
   Chlorine detectors and alarms 32
 Protection of storage vessels against overpressure 33
   Relief system 33
   Bursting discs 34
   Arrangements for relief systems 34
   Expansion vessels 37
   Pressure alarms 37
 Arrangements for unloading of liquid chlorine from road tankers to storage 38
   Unloading using dry compressed air or dry nitrogen 38
   Supply of dry padding gas to the system 39
   Unloading using chlorine gas pressure 39
   Use of re-compressed chlorine vapour 39
 Chlorine vaporisers 40
   Types 40
   Regulation of throughput 41
   Methods of heating 41
   General installation 42
   Hazards 42
   Routine and emergency isolation 45
   Pressure control valve 46
   Corrosion 46
 Chlorine absorption system 47
   Vent collection system 47
   Absorption equipment 48
   Instrumentation 48
   Disposal of effluent from the chlorine absorption plant 49

Operating and maintenance procedures, training and PPE 51
Operating instructions 51
Maintenance, inspection and installation 52
   General maintenance requirements 52
   Maintenance of connections 52
   Inspection and commissioning of chlorine tank installations 53
   Inspection procedure 54
   Testing 55
Modification of the chlorine system and clearance procedures 55
Unloading of liquid chlorine from road tankers to storage 56
Use of ISO (demountable) tank containers 57
Transfer of chlorine to the consuming units 58
   Transfer of gaseous chlorine 58
   Transfer of liquid chlorine using vapour pressure 59
   Transfer of liquid chlorine by padding with dry compressed gas 59
   Transfer of liquid chlorine using a separate pumping tank 59
   Precautions 59

Training 61
  Competency and audit 62
Personal Protective Equipment (PPE) 62
  Selecting suitable respiratory protective equipment (RPE) 63

Emergency arrangements 67
Emergency equipment 68
Control of leakages 68
  Releases inside buildings 69

Appendices 71
1 Toxicological properties and first aid 71
2 Characteristics of chlorine 73
3 Relevant legislation and HSE guidance 79
4 Useful contacts and standards 91
5 Outside installations and inside installations 95
6 Procedures for discharging road tankers of chlorine 99
7 Types of vaporiser 103
8 Emergency plans 107

References 111

List of acronyms and abbreviations 119

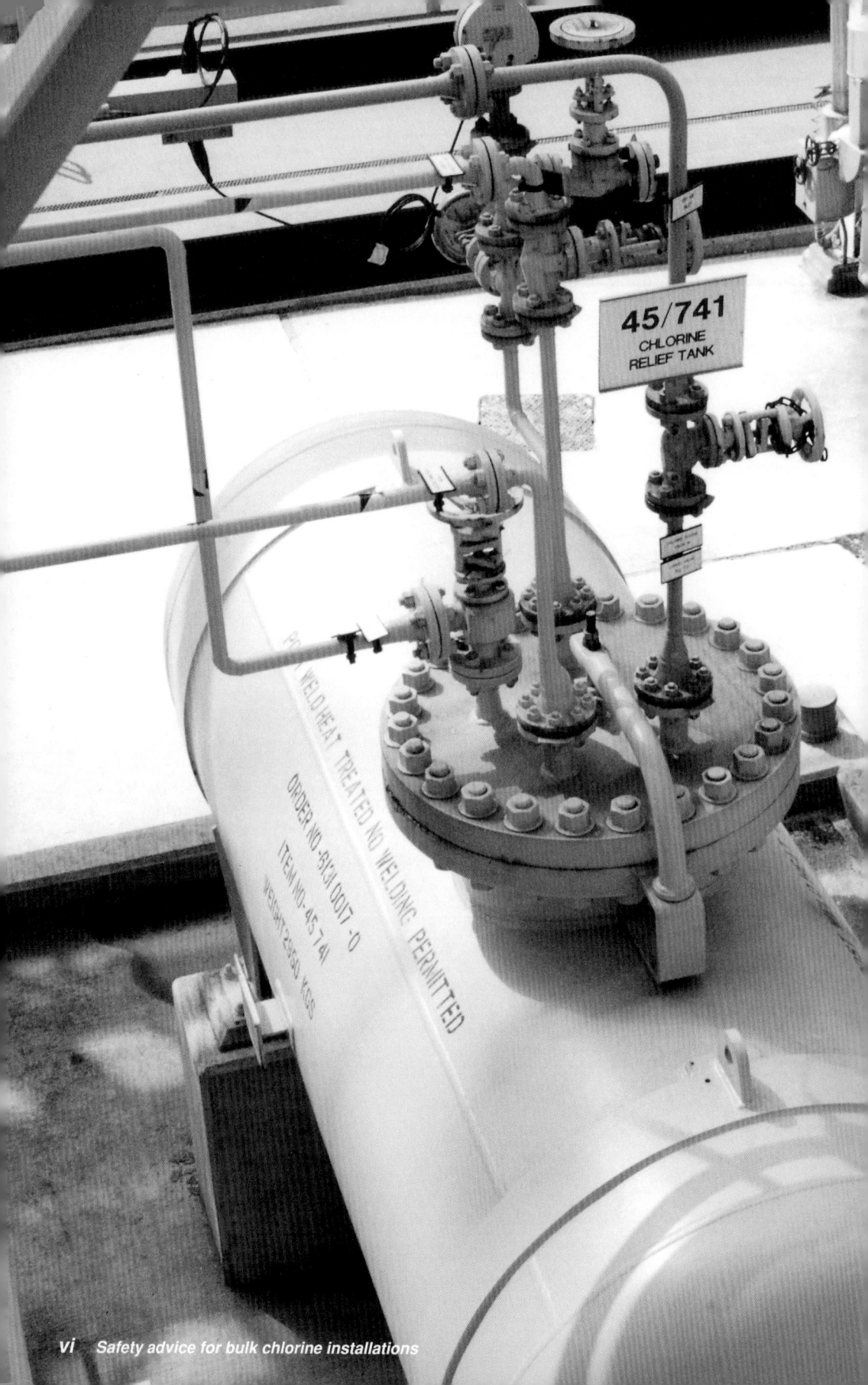

Foreword

The aim of this guidance note is to help those responsible for the safe use of chlorine from bulk containers to meet their obligations under health and safety law.

This guidance, like the document that preceded it, was prepared with the help of the chlorine producers, users, trade unions, the Water Services Association (WSA), and the Chemical Industries Association (CIA).

We are grateful to those who contributed for their assistance and co-operation in preparing this advice, and to Shaw Valves and to Descote Ltd for permission to use the photographs linked to paragraph 74, to Weston Point Studios for permission to use the photographs linked to paragraph 216 and to Zeneca plc for permission to take the remaining photographs.

The guidelines may be applied to any bulk chlorine installation but they are not intended to be a detailed design code. Some existing installations may not at present meet all the recommendations and, in some cases, not all the recommendations may be appropriate. It is for the occupier, usually in consultation with the chlorine supplier and/or specialist advisers, to judge the need for further risk control measures, following an assessment of the actual risks. If improvements are shown to be needed, a responsible decision is required from the operating company on the nature and timing of changes so that they can be made safely.

Where reference to British, European and other standards is made in this document equivalent standards are equally acceptable alternatives.

You may need help beyond that given in this guidance. If you do, trade and employer associations, such as the Chemical Industries Association and Euro Chlor, or your chlorine supplier can offer a range of advice and support. These and other sources of information are given in Appendix 4.

Introduction

1 This publication gives guidance on the safe handling of bulk liquid chlorine at sites which receive liquid chlorine by road or rail tanker, or by ISO tank container. The guidance is aimed primarily at managers of these installations, but it is also relevant for plant supervisors, design and maintenance engineers, and safety professionals. Application of the guidance will help to ensure that the risks to people on-site and off-site are minimised so far as is reasonably practicable.

2 The risks arise because chlorine is a highly toxic (see Appendix 1) and reactive substance (see Appendix 2). It forms flammable and explosive mixtures with some organic and inorganic substances. When released from containment it forms a gas cloud that is heavier than air and which maintains contact with the ground as it disperses, possibly endangering people in its path.

3 Despite the serious toxic and reactive hazards, and the potential to harm people off-site, the chlorine industry has established a very good safety record. This has been achieved through the development and practice of effective procedures for handling chlorine safely. This guidance, like the document it replaces, is issued to help maintain and enhance that record. Guidance on the safe handling of chlorine supplied in drums and cylinders is given elsewhere. [1]

4 The guidance is based on the combined experience of the four UK manufacturers of chlorine, their customers, trade unions and associations and HSE. It covers the safety and health requirements at all stages, from the receipt of the liquid chlorine to the point of use, including the location, design, testing, operation and maintenance of equipment. Procedures for dealing with emergencies are also outlined.

Management of health and safety and risk assessment

5   Employers have a legal responsibility under Sections 2 and 3 of the Health and Safety at Work etc Act 1974 (HSW Act)[2] to ensure, so far as is reasonably practicable, the health and safety of their employees and others who may be affected by their activities. Other people, such as designers, installers and suppliers, also have similar duties under the HSW Act with respect to products. Since 1974 various regulations have been made requiring specific controls for particular hazards (eg pressure systems), or activities (eg manual handling). A list of these and other current health and safety legislation, codes of practice and guidance is published annually.[3] This list also covers amendments to the regulations. References in this document are to the base regulations. Appendix 3 gives an overview of the main legislation and regulations relating to the safe handling of chlorine.

6   You must obtain planning permission for new installations in the usual way from the Local Planning Authority, who will, when appropriate, refer to HSE for advice. If you store, or plan to store, more than 10 tonnes of chlorine, your site will be subject to a number of specific regulations.

7   The Notification of Installations Handling Hazardous Substances Regulations 1982[4] require you to notify your activity to HSE if more than 10 tonnes of chlorine is liable to be kept. You must also notify subsequent changes to your activity. New installations over 10 tonnes chlorine capacity, or proposals to increase the notified capacity to more than three times the original capacity, must be notified three months in advance. The form of the notification is in the Regulations.

8   The Control of Industrial Major Accident Hazards Regulations 1984 (CIMAH)[5] also apply to sites storing or processing chlorine. These regulations apply at two levels. The lower level requirements apply to sites which store 10 or more tonnes. They also apply at sites where chlorine is involved in a process in any quantity, unless the process operation is incapable of producing a major accident hazard. You need to comply with two general requirements:

(a)   to demonstrate to HSE, at any time, that major accident hazards have been identified and adequately controlled; and

(b)   to report any major accidents to HSE.

For sites which store 75 or more tonnes, or which process chlorine and have inventories of 25 or more tonnes, unless the process operation is incapable of producing a major accident hazard, more stringent regulations apply. These require the preparation of a safety report, the preparation of on-site and off-site emergency plans and the provision of information to members of the public likely to be affected by a major accident. CIMAH will be replaced in February 1999 by the Control of Major Accident Hazard Regulations (COMAH) which implement the requirements of the Seveso II Directive[6] on the control of major accident hazards; the threshold for the lower tier requirements is 10 tonnes, and 25 tonnes for the top tier.

9   The Planning (Hazardous Substances) Regulations 1992[7] apply to sites with 10 or more tonnes of chlorine. Under these regulations the 'consent' of the local Hazardous Substances Authority (HSA) is needed for the presence of chlorine in such quantities. The HSA must consult HSE on the associated risk levels. To quantify the off-site risks HSE may request technical information about the installation.[8]

10   In addition, any process which involves the manufacture or use of chlorine or any process which is likely to result in the release of chlorine into the air or water, is a prescribed process under the Environmental Protection (Prescribed Processes and Substances) Regulations 1991.[9] Other processes are also prescribed in the Regulations. Under the Environmental Protection Act 1990[10] no person shall carry on a prescribed process except under an authorisation granted by the enforcing authority and in accordance with the conditions in the authorisation. Applications for the authorisation of a prescribed process in England and Wales must be made to the Environment Agency (EA) and in Scotland to the Scottish Environmental Protection Agency (SEPA). In addition in Scotland where the Alkali and Works Regulation Act 1906,[11] as amended by the Health and Safety (Emissions into Atmosphere) Regulations 1983,[12] is still in force, such processes are listed as Scheduled works and must be registered annually with SEPA.

11   If you fill containers from your bulk installation and transport them off-site, you will need to comply with the Carriage of Dangerous Goods (Classification, Packaging and Labelling) and Use of Transportable Pressure Receptacles Regulations 1996,[13] and the Carriage of Dangerous Goods By Road Regulations 1996[14] (in the case of transportation by road). The relevant legislation is outlined in an HSE booklet.[15] Note: The (legal) term for gas cylinders is now 'transportable pressure receptacles'.

12   Although you must comply with health and safety legislation, regulatory control cannot compensate for deficiencies in the way that safety is managed. Effective health and safety management is mainly about management (at all levels) taking a proactive approach to minimise the chance of incidents occurring rather than putting things right after they have gone wrong . Guidance on effective health and safety management is given elsewhere[16, 17] which advocates and elaborates on the following general principles of good management practice:

(a)   set your policy and demonstrate commitment to it;

(b)   organise and train your staff to ensure effective communications, co-operation, and their competence to control risks;

MANAGEMENT OF HEALTH AND SAFETY AND RISK ASSESSMENT

(c) plan what you need to do, set performance standards, and establish systems and procedures for controlling risks;

(d) measure your performance to assess whether the risks are being adequately controlled;

(e) conduct safety audits to ensure that your systems are working as intended; review your findings and take any corrective action.

A risk assessment is essential to this proactive approach to safety management and is a statutory requirement of the Management of Health and Safety at Work (MHSW) Regulations 1992.[18] Guidance on these Regulations and risk assessment is contained in an Approved Code of Practice.[19]

RISK ASSESSMENT

13   The MHSW Regulations require you to conduct a full risk assessment to identify all the hazards and assess the associated risks. The risk assessment needs to include all sources of hazards, including those associated with transport around the site, access to plant and security. The need for risk assessment is also a requirement of other regulations (eg The Control of Substances Hazardous to Health Regulations 1994 (COSHH)[20] and the Fire Precautions (Workplace) Regulations 1997.[21]

14   In outline, a risk assessment for your chlorine operations requires you to:

(a) look for the hazards ie potential sources of chlorine releases;

(b) decide how serious each of these loss-of-containment events could be, ie who could be harmed and how seriously;

(c) decide the likely frequency of each of these hazardous events;

(d) evaluate the associated risks and consider whether the precautions to prevent releases of chlorine and to mitigate their effects are adequate, or if more should be done (this guidance and the sources of advice listed in Appendix 4 is relevant here; particularly the publications of Euro Chlor;[22]

(e) record your significant findings; this is a statutory requirement if you have five or more employees; and

(f) update your risk assessment at least every three years, and before making significant modifications. Check that your operational experience accords with any significant assumptions you made to carry out your risk assessment. Safety audits, as well as day-to-day management arrangements, should address the need to check assumptions.

15 Each site will have its own special features and you need to take these into account when conducting your risk assessment. A proper risk assessment will help you to:

(a) decide whether the risks are being controlled so far as is reasonably practicable; and, if not, to:

(b) establish adequate controls and safe working procedures based on the advice in this note.

16 Your risk assessment will need to consider the main potential causes of releases of chlorine. For bulk chlorine installations these are (see paragraph 20):

(a) plant damage caused by external sources (vehicles, hoists, flying debris from nearby accidents, fires etc);

(b) incorrect operation; and

(c) inadequate inspection and maintenance.

17 The people conducting your risk assessment must have relevant experience and knowledge. If necessary, you must[18] seek assistance from experienced and knowledgeable people. Your chlorine supplier will be able to identify competent people able to conduct the risk assessment on your behalf, and supply information to help you carry out your risk assessment and to manage safety.

18 The remaining sections of this booklet provide guidance on the arrangements for prevention and mitigation of chlorine leaks and spillages through good design, operation (including emergency procedures) and maintenance. The guidance applies only to installations storing liquid chlorine under pressure in bulk tanks or tank containers. You should therefore pay particular attention to the requirements of the Pressure System and Transportable Gas Container Regulations 1989 (PSTGC).[23] Precautions for the storage of liquid chlorine in refrigerated tanks at low pressure are outside the scope of this guidance. Additional sources of advice and information are listed in Appendix 4.

Design and location of installations

19   Bulk chlorine installations operate under pressure. Consequently, the design, installation and operation (including periodic examination and maintenance) of these pressure systems will need to meet the requirements of PSTGC.[23] Pipework, equipment and protective devices for liquid chlorine are part of the system. The regulations do not apply to systems operating at or below pressures of 0.5 bar gauge, except for steam systems. Guidance on PSTGC is contained in an Approved Code of Practice[24] and the publication *A guide to the Pressure Systems and Transportable Gas Containers Regulations 1989*;[25] see Appendix 3 for brief details.

POTENTIAL INCIDENTS

20   When designing or modifying your installation, you should include provisions to prevent the following potential incidents which could result in a release of chlorine:

(a)   Damage to chlorine lines from external sources eg by hoists or vehicles - including the road tanker while it is moving to or from the unloading point. When the tanker is positioned for unloading you need to provide adequate clearance for the valve dome when it is open. You also need to make allowance for movement of the delivery vehicle during the transfer operation, eg the normal upward movement of the tanker on its suspension can cause damage if there is inadequate flexibility in the connection, or movement caused by inadequate braking or wheel chocking or careless operation by the driver.

(b)   Damage to the liquid chlorine delivery vehicle, storage tank or connecting pipework caused by impact from other vehicles.

(c)   Joint and gasket failures due to failure to tighten joints, over-tightening of joints, incorrectly fitted or the use of unsuitable joint rings, or the use of hydrocarbon based lubricants which may burn when attacked by chlorine (see Appendix 2).

(d) Errors in operating procedures, including over-filling of the storage tank and overloading of the vent scrubber, failure to close valves when removing containers, or breaking into the system for maintenance.

(e) Plant and equipment failure due to inadequate maintenance, eg 'passing' valves, or leaks caused by corrosion or erosion, or use of plant and equipment beyond the recommended life.

(f) Damage caused by fire or explosion.

SITING OF INSTALLATIONS

21   The guidance in this section relates to general features which affect the location of the installation. More specific factors are reviewed in the detailed sections dealing with off-loading (see paragraphs 134-147) and emergency procedures (see paragraphs 247-263). When deciding the location of your installation an important consideration is the potential risks to people and the environment. These risks decrease as the separation distance increases. The size of such separation distances will depend upon a number of factors, including:

(a) the number and size of storage tanks;

(b) whether the storage is indoors or outside;

(c) the operational conditions and the type of process;

(d) the frequency of chlorine deliveries;

(e) the design of the installation, eg length and diameter of liquid and vapour lines; and

(f) the size, distribution, and type (eg sensitive groups) of the surrounding population.

22   You should carefully consider these factors when designing and deciding the location of your installation and when conducting your risk assessment (see paragraphs 13-17). You should involve your chlorine supplier at an early stage. Consideration should be given to maximising the distance between the site boundary and the chlorine installation. It should be emphasised that your risk assessment and individual circumstances (see paragraph 21) will determine the separation distances. The same considerations also apply when making significant changes to an existing installation within a site.

23   When choosing the location for your chlorine area, you need to consider the location of other on-site buildings in relation to the prevailing wind direction. It is recommended that the chlorine area should be located downwind of buildings that are regularly occupied. Ventilation intakes to occupied rooms should be at least 25 m from the chlorine installation, and preferably at a high level.

24   You also need to take account of the prevailing wind direction when deciding the locations of emergency assembly points. Two assembly points are recommended; these should be located so that at least one will be available regardless of the wind direction when a release occurs. For complex sites, indoor assembly points are recommended; open air assembly points may be suitable for simple sites.

DESIGN AND LOCATION OF INSTALLATIONS

25 For a new installation, full account will have to be taken of any requirements attached to the planning permission granted by the Planning Authority. In addition the local Planning Authority needs to ensure that the overall plan will avoid problems arising in the future from developments leading to a high density of population near the installation, or from the introduction of other potential hazards in an adjacent area (see Appendix 3: Planning (Hazardous Substances) Regulations 1992). For sites which may present such hazards HSE may recommend that the highest standards are applied, before consent can be granted by the HSA. In some cases the consideration of off-site risk levels by HSE may require control measures in addition to those recommended in this guidance.

26 For existing installations, control of neighbouring population densities is not possible in the short term. However, proposed developments nearby which would increase the number of people are controllable and would be permitted by the local Planning Authority only after detailed consideration. Such consideration will include the advice received from HSE on the risks from chlorine releases to those who may occupy or use the proposed development.

27 The location of a new chlorine installation within a site should be decided following a risk assessment. In making your decision you should take into account possible damage from flooding or subsidence, and the possible damage to the installation if neighbouring plant or factories suffer a catastrophe by fire or explosion. Installations should be sited at a sufficient distance (25 m minimum) from public roads or main railway lines to reduce the risk of damage to the installation if there is an accident. Protective barriers should be installed where necessary.

28 In all cases, suitable fences, together with adequate security supervision, should be provided to minimise the possibility of unauthorised access.

29 Hazards arising from aircraft may normally be regarded as minimal with probabilities below the level of significance required for any special consideration. However, attention may be necessary in exceptional circumstances, eg if the installation is at the end of an airport runway or close to a busy airfield. In such circumstances liaison with the airfield operator on suitable risk reduction measures is essential.

30 The installation is preferably located in the open air; but under some circumstances an indoor installation may be appropriate. In deciding this, it is important that a risk assessment is made, taking into account the factors listed in Appendix 5. You need to consider the following possible risk reduction measures at an early stage:

(a) the scope for reducing the chlorine inventory, eg rescheduling of deliveries;

(b) interlocking arrangements (see also paragraphs 35, 39-41) for the automatic isolation of leaks and to prevent the delivery vehicle moving during transfer operations;

(c) minimising the length and diameter of pipework carrying liquid chlorine and ensuring overpressure protection;

(d) mechanically ventilating chlorine buildings and discharge through a fume scrubbing system; the associated air inlet ducts should be at a low level;

(e) improving the leak-tightness of any chlorine building against major leaks; and

(f) restricting transfers of chlorine to daylight hours or normal working hours (8.00 am to 5.00 pm) as the weather conditions are likely to be more favourable for the dilution of chlorine concentrations if there is a release.

UNLOADING AREA

Design and location

31   You should aim to minimise the possibility of chlorine escape during the transfer of liquid chlorine from the delivery vehicles to the storage tank. Detailed attention to the siting, design and layout of the unloading equipment and operating procedure is essential.

32   The unloading area should be on reasonably level ground with adequate surrounding space providing good access from different directions. The location should minimise the risk of impact damage from vehicles, mobile equipment or falling objects from lifting equipment.

33   The unloading point should be reasonably close to the storage installation. To avoid impact damage a protective barrier between the tanker bay and the storage installation is recommended. The unloading point should also be sited at a safe distance from drains, rivers, drainage collection points and any plant or equipment which might give rise to fire or explosion.

34   Satisfactory access should be provided to the permanent pipework for discharge of the chlorine tankers and to ensure that connections to the tankers can be made safely. Where this involves working from a place above ground level, a permanent structure should be provided. This should be designed so that, in case of emergency, escape is possible with minimum risk. You can achieve this by installing a substantial and non-flammable (eg steel) structure and ensuring that platforms are free of obstructions and have non-slip surfaces, adequate toe-boards and guard-rails. Alternative escape ways should be provided with stairways of standard slope. Vertical ladders or steep stairways should be avoided. If vertical ladders are unavoidable, ensure that safety hoops, etc, do not impede access for people wearing breathing apparatus. The design of moveable platforms giving access to the top of the tankers needs to minimise the possibility of accidents due to collision with the tankers. Interlock systems may be used for this purpose, see paragraphs 39-41.

DESIGN AND LOCATION OF INSTALLATIONS

A well designed unloading area

35   You need to provide for the safe isolation of any leaks that may arise, particularly from pipework carrying liquid chlorine. It is recommended that remotely or automatically controlled valves should be installed on the transfer line to the storage tanks. When automatic isolation is employed, operated by chlorine sensors in the unloading area, the detector system needs to close both the storage tank isolation valve and that on the tanker. The possibility of liquid chlorine being trapped between closed valves and the need for pressure relief (see paragraphs 61-67) needs to be considered.

36   It is also good practice to provide:

(a)   protection against the weather on fixed gantries at unloading points, eg by windbreaks or overhead canopies;

(b)   storage space for connectors used for transfer operations so that they can be kept dry and protected from dirt and moisture getting in, and possible impact damage;

(c)   storage space for emergency equipment (eg filter respirators, breathing apparatus, protective clothing and spare equipment) in a safe location so that the equipment is readily available in an emergency;

(d)   adequate lighting and emergency lighting covering the unloading area, and all escape routes;

(e)   sufficient manually operated alarm stations to enable warning to be given in the event of a chlorine escape. Further details on emergency procedures are given in paragraphs 247-263.

Deliveries of liquid chlorine by road tanker or ISO tank container

37   The Carriage of Dangerous Goods (CDG) by Road Regulations 1996[14] and the CDG (Driver Training) Regulations 1996[26] apply. For safety reasons all UK road tankers are fitted with air-operated shut-off valves for the padding air (see paragraphs 134-141) and the chlorine delivery connections. It is also strongly recommended that the following means of minimising potential risks are adopted wherever possible:

(a)   Provision of a separate and protected unloading area for the sole use of chlorine tankers (eg by erecting side protection of the motorway-type crash barrier).

(b)   Restriction by suitable means of the speed of traffic on adjacent roads.

(c)   Unauthorised access of vehicles and personnel to the unloading area should be prevented, eg by placing warning barriers, notices, moveable barriers or road cones, or closing gates when the chlorine tankers are in position.

(d)   Provision of an interlock (see paragraphs 39-41) system to prevent coupling of liquid chlorine lines to the tankers and opening of the discharge valve until the tanker is immobilised. In addition, the air-operated tanker valves should be interlocked with the chlorine detection and shut-down system, or be remotely operable from the emergency stop points.

(e)   A system of work whereby one person (the driver for road deliveries) is present throughout the unloading (see paragraphs 214-215, and Appendix 6), and a second is present during connection and disconnection. The second person should be nearby and available throughout unloading to provide help on request.

(f)   Routing of chlorine pipework in the area to minimise the risk of damage from impact by the tanker, other vehicles or mobile equipment.

Tanker waiting to enter unloading area

DESIGN AND LOCATION OF INSTALLATIONS

38   Where a separate unloading area cannot be provided, and the unloading point is on a factory through road, such roads should be physically closed (see paragraph 37c) to other traffic during the transfer of liquid chlorine. Your risk assessment will determine whether additional measures are needed.

Interlocks

The discharge arm and the padding-air arm connectors cannot be released from their anchor points until the barriers are locked in position and the mechanical interlock keys removed and used to unlock the arms

39   Interlocks should be used to prevent serious incidents. For example, interlocks can be used to ensure that the vehicle brakes are fully applied before the unloading pipe is finally connected up and the tanker valve opened; or, a barrier on the unloading platform can be interlocked to the loading connector, so preventing inadvertent movement of a tanker still connected up. Alternatively the pressure in the unloading pipe can activate a flashing sign to remind the driver that the tanker is still connected (the latter system may be appropriate at a producer plant or a consumer plant with a large throughput).

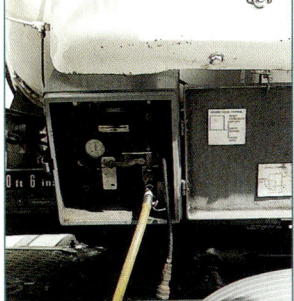

The air supply to the truck's brakes has to be disconnected before the instument air (needed to operate the tanker padding air and chlorine discharge valves) can be connected

40   The manoeuvring necessary to locate a road tanker precisely in relation to a solid pipe connector may make it more difficult to devise an interlock to the highest standard of security. In such cases, an interlock to prevent access of other tankers is strongly recommended, and special attention must be paid to the system of work which effectively prevents accidental movement of the tanker, and to driver training. Alternatively movement detectors of the light beam and reflector type can be used and interlocked to close the isolation valves and sound the audible alarm.

41   Interlocks may be used to prevent some releases due to operator error. For example to ensure that liquid chlorine is not transferred to the vent absorber, in addition to a procedure (step 9 of Appendix 6)

Safety advice for bulk chlorine installations   **13**

requiring the closure of the manual vent valve on the liquid chlorine delivery line before starting the tanker discharge procedure, the vent valve should be interlocked with the delivery point or the tanker off-loading valve.

Deliveries of liquid chlorine by rail tanker

42   The Carriage of Dangerous Goods by Rail Regulations 1996[27] apply. It is strongly recommended that you adopt the following means of minimising potential risks. Your risk assessment will determine whether additional measures are needed.

(a)   Close the sidings to other traffic during transfer of chlorine from tankers to storage, by locking the points. Alternatively, friction buffers or a de-railer may be used.

(b)   Control by suitable means the volume and speed of adjacent traffic.

(c)   Close warning barriers and/or place warning notices when the chlorine tankers are in position.

(d)   Provide an interlock (see paragraphs 39-41) system to prevent coupling or uncoupling of the liquid chlorine lines, unless barriers or warning notices are in position. It is recommended that the interlock system extends to ensure that appropriate points on the rail sidings are locked and wheel stops raised before transfer of liquid chlorine can start.

(e)   Establish a system of work whereby one person is responsible for the whole operation of unloading, and a second is within call during connection and disconnection. The second person should be in the area and available throughout unloading.

Flexible couplings to the tanker for liquid chlorine and padding air. Notice the swivel joint and the spring loaded pipework suspension for the padding air and liquid chlorine lines

(f)   Route chlorine pipelines in the area to minimise the risk of damage from collision by the tanker, other vehicles or mobile equipment.

Owing to the very limited use of rail transport, the rest of this guidance focuses on chlorine delivery by road tanker. When rail transport is used, the same general principles for the safe handling of bulk deliveries of chlorine apply.

CONNECTIONS BETWEEN THE TANKER AND THE FIXED LINES TO THE STORAGE INSTALLATION *(see also paragraphs 134 -147)*

43   To transfer liquid chlorine to storage, it is necessary to couple the liquid chlorine outlet line on the tanker to the inlet line to storage. It is also necessary to increase the tanker pressure by about 1.7 bar above that in the storage tank by connecting a supply of dry compressed air, nitrogen or chlorine vapour to the tanker. The associated pipework (see paragraphs 53-79) should be as simple as possible to minimise the risk of potential loss-of-containment accidents.

DESIGN AND LOCATION OF INSTALLATIONS

44   Connections for the transfer of liquid chlorine require very careful consideration, as they are a potential source of loss-of-containment leading to a release of chlorine to the environment. Failure of the unloading connections can result from inadequate design, poor weather protection, incorrect materials of construction, inadequate pipework support, improper use, or inadequate inspection and maintenance. Therefore, you need to ensure that the design standards are adequate, that testing and inspection procedures are regularly carried out and that the equipment is satisfactorily maintained.

Types of connection

45   Three types of connection are available:

(a)   Flexible couplings (sometimes called semi-rigid loading arms) have:

   (i)   a solid connection pipe with swivel joints to facilitate connection to the tanker; and

   (ii) a degree of flexibility built into the supports and hanger to allow movement when coupled up, ie a cranked free length of pipe or a coiled pipe.

(b)   Flexible hoses.

(c)   Articulated arms.

Flexible couplings are normally used, but flexible hoses or articulated arms may be used by agreement with, or recommendation of, the chlorine supplier.

Flexible couplings (semi-rigid loading arms)

46   Flexible couplings are normally constructed from steel pipe. However, Hastelloy C (not B) pipe is recommended up to the first isolation valve. This offers greater life in situations where the pipe is repeatedly exposed to very small amounts of atmospheric moisture by the connection/disconnection process. Flexibility is provided by a cranked free length of pipe (less usually by a coil) to allow for vertical movement of the tanker during discharge. Screwed connections are used for the connections to the road tanker; screwed connections to BS21[28] are commonly used at either end of the flexible coupling. 'Swivel' joints in the padding gas line and the liquid chlorine line facilitate connection to the tanker. These joints are tightened once the connections are made. Flanged connections are used for connecting to rail tankers.

47   Piping local to the tanker berth should not be fixed for the first 5-7 m but it needs to be supported. The system of support used should ensure that the pipework is kept above the headroom required by the tanker when it is being put in position. The support should also allow the pipework sufficient vertical movement to accommodate that in the delivery vehicle's suspension system during the unloading operation - typically about 150 mm. A minimum internal pipe diameter of 25 mm is recommended.

48   The design criteria for flexible couplings constructed from pipework are similar to those for fixed pipework (see paragraphs 56-60). Where the connections are screwed connections, the gasket should be a trapped joint ring, which is renewed at every connection (see also paragraph 215).

Flexible hoses

49   The design of flexible hoses[29, 30] should be agreed with your chlorine supplier. They require more frequent testing than flexible couplings and their life is shorter, but positioning of tankers is easier. Flexible Monel braided hose connections are normally constructed up to 50 mm (2 in) size for the liquid chlorine discharge, and 25 mm (1 in) size for the compressed gas connection to the tanker.

50   The operating instructions covering unloading should ensure that visual inspection and leak testing of the flexible hoses is carried out before commencing transfer of liquid chlorine (see also paragraph 215).

Articulated arms

51   Articulated arms, with swivelled joints (knuckles), are usually used on high volume installations. They should be designed to meet the requirements specified in the Euro Chlor publication GEST 75/44[31] and certified as meeting this or an equivalent standard. They should be operated and maintained as advised by the manufacturer. Arms should be visually inspected for defects and tested for gas tightness every time they are used. Suspect arms should be immediately withdrawn from service for maintenance.

52   Where the seals at knuckle joints are purged by a flow of dry (dew point less than -40°C) air or nitrogen, this gas should be continuously sampled by a chlorine detector system with an alarm. An isolation valve suitable for use with articulated arms should be attached to the discharge end of the arm to prevent air entering the arm after operation. It should:

(a)   ensure a gas tight seal when the arm is not in use to prevent moisture getting in - an end cap should also be used; and

(b)   permit the venting down of the arm and depressurisation of any connection adapter. The arm should be vented after each operation and purged with a suitable dry gas.

When an arm is out of service the purge gas should be maintained under a small pressure (eg 0.5 bar gauge).

You need to keep a register showing each operation and the quantity (eg tonnes) of chlorine transferred.

PIPEWORK FOR LIQUID CHLORINE

53 In designing your pipework you should take steps to guard against the following causes of failure:

(a) impact;

(b) heating, eg fire (resulting in a reaction between the steel and chlorine);

(c) severe internal or external corrosion;

(d) overpressure (see paragraphs 61-67); and

(e) erosion due to relatively high liquid velocities and inadequate inspection and maintenance procedures. Liquid velocities less than 2 m/s are recommended.

54 Routing of pipework for liquid chlorine should normally be above ground and should be such as to maximise protection from mechanical damage, corrosion and fire. A minimum internal diameter of 25 mm (1 in) is recommended to ensure adequate mechanical strength.

Permanent pipework at the unloading point

55 The permanent pipework at the unloading point usually consists of the following lines:

(a) pipework for pressurising the tanker with dry air, nitrogen or chlorine (see also paragraph 134-147);

(b) pipework for the transfer of liquid chlorine to storage; and

(c) pipework for instrument air lines, eg to operate the remotely controlled valves on the tanker.

The source of compressed 'padding' air needs to be independent from that supplying other services. Detailed design requirements for the pipework and fittings are described in paragraphs 56-79. The system for off-loading of liquid chlorine is described in paragraphs 134-147.

Design criteria for pipework transferring liquid chlorine to storage tanks or from storage to point of use

56 Your pipework will be part of a pressure system and subject to the requirements of the PSTGC Regulations.[23-25] It therefore needs to be properly designed, fabricated, inspected and tested in accordance with a recognised Code, eg ANSI/ASME B31.3[32, 33] and should be sufficiently robust for all foreseeable conditions of work.

(a) Design pressure. Should not be less than 12 bar gauge (174 psig), corresponding to a design temperature of +45 °C. Any part of the system which may operate at a higher temperature should be designed to withstand the corresponding vapour pressure (see Appendix 2, Figure A2.1).

(b) Design temperature. Should be less than the minimum at which the pipe is intended to operate, or the temperature to which it will be cooled if liquid chlorine boils off at atmospheric pressure (-35°C). The normal design range is -35°C to +45°C. In certain uncommon situations lower temperatures are possible due to chlorine cooling below its boiling point, eg when purging systems with dry gas - locations where liquid chlorine has collected may cool to temperatures as low -50°C due to evaporative cooling. Your chlorine supplier should be able to provide advice on the need to design for such low temperatures.

(c) Materials of construction. Care is needed in selecting suitable materials (see Appendix 2). Seamless carbon steel tubing is recommended for pipework. All components of pipes, valves and fittings should be resistant to the action of chlorine between the extremes of operating temperatures and pressures. Original material certificates should be kept throughout the plant's life.

(d) Corrosion allowance. 1 mm.

(e) Radius of curvature of any formed bends. Three pipe diameters minimum (weld elbows must be used where tighter bends are necessary). Elbows, tees and reducing pieces should be forged or hot-formed without reduction in wall thickness.

(f) Bolting. Should be designed to the requirements of BS 4882.[34]

(g) Flanges. The number of flanges should be limited as far as possible and those used should be to the requirements of a recognised design code eg BS 1560[35] or ASME/ANSI B16-5.[36] Steel used for fabrication of flanges or welded connections to the pipe must be compatible with that of the pipe itself.

(h) Gaskets. The use of incorrect materials for gaskets can be dangerous; if in doubt you should seek the advice of your chlorine supplier. Rubber gaskets should never be used for liquid chlorine service. All packings, gaskets and diaphragms should be resistant to the action of chlorine between the extremes of operating temperatures and pressures. Proven materials such as spiral wound Monel, Kel-F or Aramid fibre are suitable. Compressed asbestos fibre (CAF) gaskets to BS 1832,[37] grade A or O, preferably graphite-treated on each face to facilitate dismantling, are suitable for joints that are expected to remain in service for several years without being disturbed. Any used asbestos components should be collected and disposed of safely. Where joints are made and remade relatively frequently CAF is not recommended for environmental reasons. Alternative jointing material such as aramid fibre should be used. Polytetrafluoroethylene (PTFE) to BS 6564[38] grade UA 1/1 may be suitable provided the joint is of an encapsulated type (eg a spigotted joint) to prevent the PTFE 'creeping'. Some users have found lead to be suitable on small diameter pipework (less than 25 mm). Where a variety of gasket materials are used joints should be tabbed for easy identification.

(i) Manufacturers' instructions need to be strictly adhered to. Avoid over-tightening fittings as this can result in leaks due to the subsequent failure of the fixing nuts or packing.

(j) Lubrication. Normally in assembling pipe flanges, bolts and gaskets, no lubricants are required. Where lubrication is needed, only fully inert oils and greases recommended for chlorine duty should be used. On no account must hydrocarbon-based lubricants be used as they react with chlorine and may ignite. The heat generated may be sufficient to cause a chlorine-iron fire (see Appendix 2) which would result in a pipework failure and a release of chlorine.

57 The following controls should be applied during construction:

(a) Stress relief. All fabricated items and butt welds should be stress-relieved before final inspection and testing.

(b) Inspection and pressure testing. All weld spatter, scale and other foreign matter should be removed. All butt welds should be fully radiographed or ultrasonically examined. All pipework should be pressure-tested in accordance with the design code. Where hydrostatic tests are made it is essential that the complete piping system is thoroughly cleaned and dried to a dew point less than -40°C before introducing chlorine. All traces of oil, grease and solvents must be removed (eg with steam or aqueous detergents or both) for the reasons stated under 'Lubrication' in paragraph 56. If a hydrostatic test is made after installation it will be necessary to change all gaskets to ensure dryness. Appropriate leak tests will then be required to check the newly made joints.

(c) Modifications. Any extension, modification or repairs to pipework should be carried out to a standard at least equivalent to the original design and construction code including stress relief, inspection and testing.

Protection of pipework

58 You should install pipework conveying chlorine so that it is:

(a) protected from impact by vehicles by distance or with barriers;

(b) protected from falling objects eg no overhead hoists. Canopy roofs for weather protection should be constructed of lightweight materials;

(c) separated from pipework carrying corrosive or flammable materials or other sources of heat, eg steam - the separation will depend on the nature of the other material and an estimate of the hazard;

(d) adequately supported;

(e) accessible for maintenance and inspection;

(f) preferably unlagged; and

(g) regularly inspected under any lagging to detect corrosion due to failure of weather-sealing.

Marking

59   The chlorine area needs to be clearly identified, marked[39-41] - see also the Dangerous Substances Regulations in Appendix 3 - and secured against unauthorised entry. It is recommended that chlorine pipework should be clearly labelled and painted yellow in accordance with BS 1710[42] (eg to 08E51-BS 4800[43]). The Health and Safety (Safety Signs and Signals) Regulations 1996[44] require clear labelling whenever risks to employees cannot be avoided or adequately reduced by other means; advice is given in the associated guidance.[45]

60   It is good practice to mark valves which are required to operate in an emergency. They should be marked with a clear indication of their function and the direction in which they open and close. These markings need to be consistent with the markings on any flow diagrams or operational instructions. Valve keys for operating the emergency valves should be located near to the valve.

PROTECTION OF LIQUID CHLORINE PIPEWORK AGAINST OVERPRESSURE

61   Trapping of liquid chlorine between closed valves, followed by a rise in temperature, increases the risk of overpressure. Even a small temperature rise can cause a very high hydraulic pressure, because of the high coefficient of expansion of liquid chlorine (see Appendix 2).

62   The risk of liquid chlorine being trapped between closed valves is increased by the following factors:

(a) Isolation valves that are controlled by different operators. This may be a special risk where there are long lines or complex pipework between units.

(b) The simultaneous closure of automatically operated valves that have been installed for plant isolation. This risk should be assessed. In some circumstances it may be preferable to employ at least one manually initiated remotely controlled valve.

63   You should design your system and operating procedures to minimise the risks of overpressurisation. When appropriate, pressure relief devices should be fitted.

Provision of relief systems

64   Relief systems complicate pipework and introduce other potential hazards, and should in general be avoided. However, if the capacity of your system is such that release of the chlorine present could lead to a serious incident, automatic means of releasing excessive pressure in the pipework needs to be provided. It follows that the configuration of the pipework, positioning of valves, and valve-closing methods (see paragraph 62) have to be studied to see whether the hazard can occur.

65   Pressure relief systems should be designed to meet your operating conditions. It is recommended that the need for, and the design of, relief systems is fully discussed with your chlorine supplier.

66   A common method of pressure relief for protection of liquid chlorine lines is via a bursting disc installed in a vertical tee on the pipework, discharging to a suitable collecting system (see Figure 1) The relief volume of the pressure vessel should be at least 20% of the line volume. Any expansion vessel should be registered as a pressure vessel for examination and recording purposes.[23]

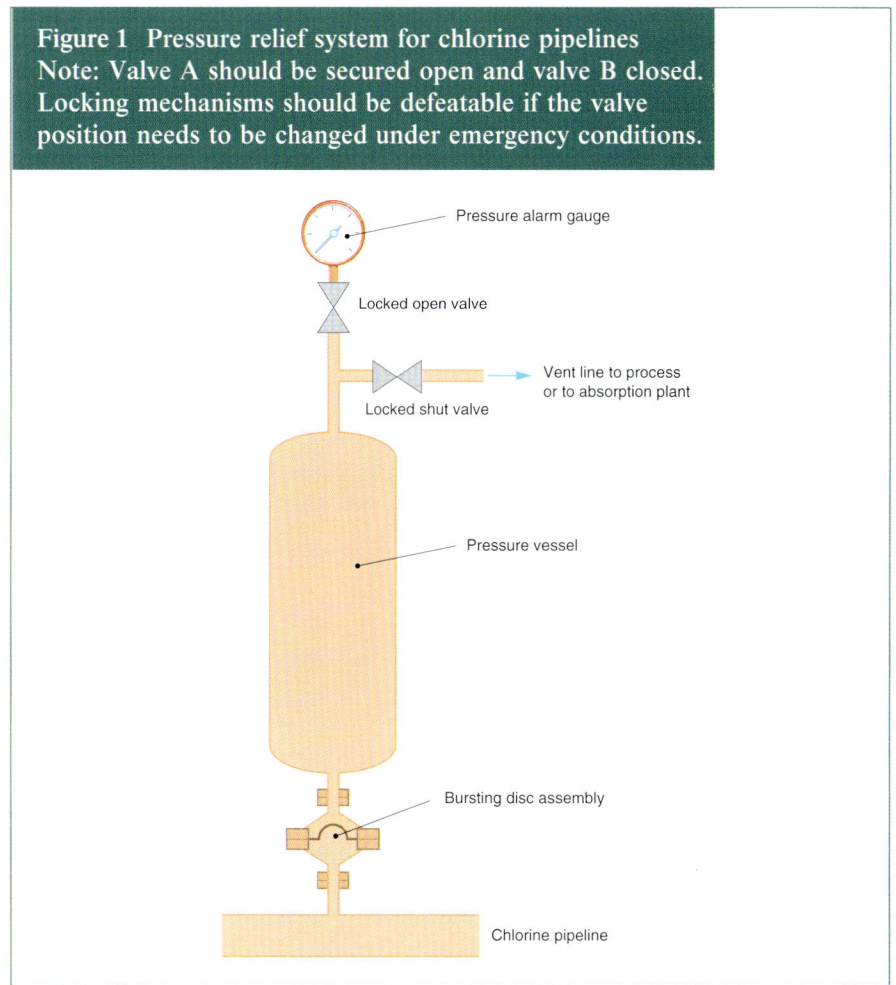

Figure 1 Pressure relief system for chlorine pipelines
Note: Valve A should be secured open and valve B closed. Locking mechanisms should be defeatable if the valve position needs to be changed under emergency conditions.

67   The pressure vessel should be fitted with a suitable alarm which operates as a result of the rise in pressure in the vessel, if the bursting disc leaks or ruptures. The vessel and line can then be vented to process, or to the chlorine absorption system via a normally locked-closed valve. The heated 'bottle' system originally used on older installations is now obsolete and not recommended.

VALVES

68   It is strongly recommended that Euro Chlor approved valves are used on new installations. Care is essential in the choice of valves (eg see the publications on valves in reference 22) as they have to be resistant to chlorine and able to cope with the stresses to which they may be subjected. The valve body should preferably be made of forged steel; cast iron is not acceptable. If the valve design is such that liquid chlorine could be trapped within the body when the valve is closed, provision should be made to avoid excess pressure which may develop with temperature rise. In other situations the evaporation of liquid chlorine may cause operating temperatures to fall below -35°C (see paragraph 56(b)); the valves should be selected so as not to fail if this occurs. Problems which are specific to cold or to liquid chlorine limit the application of certain designs of valve.

69   The selection of the appropriate type of valve for each application should be reviewed with your chlorine supplier who will be able to suggest manufacturers of valves whose equipment has given satisfactory service with liquid chlorine. This will reduce the possibility of unsatisfactory valves being used which will require replacement after a short period and could be a potential source of hazard.

70   Valves which are 'permanently' open (eg to prevent inadvertent isolation of pressure alarms), or 'permanently' closed (eg emergency vent lines) should be secured in these positions. The locking mechanisms should be capable of being broken in the event of an emergency, eg the lead or plastic seal type.

71   It is emphasised that, during maintenance operations, reliance on valves of whatever type for isolation is insufficient. The design of the system should be such that complete isolation of the section concerned is possible. Suitable methods for achieving this include the installation of spool pieces in the lines which can be removed and substituted by blanks, or the insertion of slip plates.[46]

Types of valve

72   Valves of the following types have been developed for use with liquid chlorine or dry chlorine gas under pressure:

(a)   vertical globe valves;

(b)   conical plug valves;

(c)   ball valves.

73   Valves have to be degreased using steam or detergents and then completely dried before use. All traces of any solvent used should be removed as it could react with chlorine (see paragraph 57(b)). It is recommended that after this treatment the valves should be stored in individual gas-tight plastic bags ready for installation when required.

Vertical globe valves

74   This type of valve is preferred to other types and is used for isolation of liquid chlorine stock tanks or for large flows of chlorine gas. The billet-globe valve is recommended for installation on the liquid chlorine outlet line from chlorine storage tanks (see paragraph 96). The gas seal around the valve spindle in globe valves may be formed by a packed gland (preferably using rings or chevrons of PTFE) or by a bellows seal. The bellows should be backed up by a secondary gland seal. Globe valves may, with advantage, be fitted with a back seating arrangement which isolates the gland from line pressure when the valve is fully open.

Gland packed globe valve
(typical sizes available 15mm to 250mm)

Bellows sealed globe valve with pneumatic actuator. Hydraulic and electrical actuators are also available

Angle pattern globe valve

Conical plug valves (PTFE-sleeved)

75   Conical plug valves, PTFE-sleeved, are satisfactory for isolation of liquid chlorine lines, particularly when quick isolation may be required, but the primary valve on the storage tank is preferably a globe valve. Rapid isolation can cause pressure surges and you need to consider these when designing your installation (see also paragraph 79).

76   Conical plug valves for use with liquid chlorine require provision for the avoidance of problems arising from liquid chlorine trapped in the bore when the valve is closed. If this makes the valves uni-directional, they need to be marked with an indication of the required direction of liquid flow to ensure correct installation. Gas-tightness is provided by a PTFE sleeve inserted into the body of the valve and by a supplementary seal along the length of the spindle between the valve body and head. Care should be taken to avoid the application of side thrust to the spindles of plug valves.

Ball valves

77   This type of valve can be used for isolation in liquid chlorine lines and should incorporate the following:

(a)   spherical turning limited to a quarter-turn;

(b)   straight-through flanging;

(c)   PTFE seals.

78   Ball valves should be avoided when operating conditions involve large and frequent temperature changes. If used with liquid chlorine, you should make provision for avoiding problems arising from liquid chlorine trapped in the bore when the valve is closed. Liquid trapped in the ball should be released downstream via a small hole in the ball. If this makes the valve uni-directional it needs to be marked with an indication of the required direction of liquid flow to ensure correct installation. (Ball valves may not seal when the sealing pressure and the system pressure are in opposite directions). The remarks about pressure surges in paragraphs 75 and 79 also apply.

Remotely controlled valves

79   The rate of closure of any actuated valve should not be so rapid that it causes undue pressure surges in the system. The standard rate of closure should be satisfactory for pipework up to 50 mm diameter. Long runs of larger diameter pipework may require lower rates of closure to prevent liquid hammer. You should seek advice from your valve supplier.

STORAGE VESSELS *(see also paragraphs 190-229)*

80   To minimise the danger of over-filling your storage vessel, its capacity needs to be significantly greater than that of the largest delivery vehicle. The chosen capacity will depend on the rate of consumption and the frequency of deliveries. Installation of bulk storage facilities should be considered only if the annual consumption of chlorine is sufficient to justify bulk supplies rather than purchase of liquid chlorine in drums or ISO containers (see paragraphs 216-221). An installation consisting of smaller tanks which would require split loads is not recommended. New sites should involve HSE at an early stage.

81   In considering the number of individual storage tanks for a required total storage capacity, take the following points into account:

(a)   The minimum working capacity of the tank should be adequate to safely accommodate the working stock residue and the maximum foreseen unit delivery.

(b)   If continuity of supply is essential, at least two tanks will be required to allow time for necessary inspections and to facilitate maintenance. This also provides greater flexibility of operation.

(c)   Increasing the number of storage tanks leads to an increase in the ancillary plant and equipment with a corresponding increase in complexity of operation.

DESIGN AND LOCATION OF INSTALLATIONS

82 The distance between adjacent storage tanks should be adequate to provide good access to the tanks under all circumstances. This includes those in which bulky protective equipment (such as self-contained breathing apparatus) is being used.

Chlorine storage vessel and bund. Note the emergency stop button (one of several) at the edge of the bund.

83 All chlorine storage tanks should be installed in a bund which is impervious to liquid chlorine. The bund should be capable of taking the contents of the largest storage tank with adequate freeboard and a sump. If there is a sub-division to give a separate section under each tank, each section should have a sloping floor leading to a sump, which may serve more than one tank. Sumps should not be connected to the drain. Provision should be included for removal of rain water over the bund wall, not via the drain or through valves in the bund.

84 Leaks of liquid chlorine are potentially much more dangerous than leaks of gaseous chlorine. Your system therefore needs to be designed so that sources of leakage of liquid are reduced to a minimum, eg by avoiding joints which are continuously exposed to liquid chlorine such as bottom outlets, see paragraph 88.

85 The severity of a leak is reduced by lowering the pressure within the system and therefore it is important that facilities for transferring gaseous chlorine to a consuming process or to a waste-chlorine absorption plant are available. You should also consider in your risk assessment the need for arrangements to transfer liquid chlorine from a leaking tank to another tank which can be isolated.

86 Layout of the chlorine area should be planned to provide all facilities necessary for good housekeeping and emergency response. Chlorine storage tanks should therefore be erected above ground level. Installation in deep pits is not recommended because it increases the difficulties of treatment and dispersal of a chlorine escape and of access for maintenance or repair. Ample storage space is needed for maintenance and safety equipment, which has to be readily accessible in an emergency.

87 Thermal insulation of the storage tanks is not normally required. However, if your vessel is relatively close to a fire hazard and lagging is required, the material should be fire-resistant, chemically inert to liquid or gaseous chlorine and resistant to atmospheric moisture getting in. Periodic inspection beneath the lagging is essential when checking for corrosion.

Design criteria

88 Design criteria for new liquid chlorine storage and expansion vessels are outlined below.

(a) Design pressure. 12 bar gauge (174 psig) minimum.

(b) Design temperature. When liquid chlorine evaporates at atmospheric pressure its temperature falls to -35°C and therefore the minimum design temperature should not be any higher, but lower temperatures are possible if evaporative cooling of liquid chlorine occurs, see paragraph 56(b). The normal design range is -35°C to +45°C.

(c) Filling ratio. Filling ratios for transportable liquid chlorine containers are detailed in BS 5355[47] for various size ranges of mobile containers and for different temperatures. Although there is no equivalent standard for fixed tanks, for simplicity a figure of 1.25 kg of liquid chlorine/litre capacity is normally used to fix the maximum level to which the tank may be filled and the setting chosen for the high level alarm. This ensures that the volume of liquid chlorine does not exceed 95% of the total volume of the vessel, even for a maximum temperature of 50°C.

(d) Design code. New vessels should be designed and manufactured to BS 5500[48] Category 1 (or an equivalent standard).

(e) Corrosion allowance. Minimum 1 mm.

(f) Supports and load cells. The vessel supports should be designed in accordance with the design code to permit thermal expansion or contraction over the design temperature range. Special consideration may be necessary (check with your supplier) where load cells are used for determining the contents of the tank, eg certain types of weighing device require secondary supports.

(g) Branches. Dimensions should be limited to the minimum required, particularly for the liquid lines. All branches should be mounted, where possible, on the manhole cover or covers. Manhole access should be provided on top of the vessel. The opening should preferably be 600 mm diameter, but in no case should it be less than 460 mm diameter. Bottom outlets should not be provided except where required for chlorine transfer by pumping. Any bottom outlet should have an internal valve, preferably remotely-operable, plus a back-up isolating valve (see paragraph 97).

(h) Bolting. Should meet the requirements of BS 4882.[34]

(i) Gaskets. Use of incorrect materials for gaskets can be dangerous, see paragraph 56(h) for suitable materials.

(j) Documentation. Regulation 5 of PSTGC[23-25] requires designers, manufacturers and suppliers of pressure systems to provide sufficient written information concerning the design, construction, examination, operation and maintenance to enable the regulations to be complied with. You must retain this information together with any Certificate of Compliance (eg BS 5500[48] or similar documentation if other standards are being used).

DESIGN AND LOCATION OF INSTALLATIONS

(k) Marking. The vessel must be marked with the details specified in Schedule 4 of the PSTGC Regulations. All valves and pipework associated with chlorine storage tanks should be labelled and colour coded (see also paragraphs 59 and 60).

89 Paragraph 88 applies to new systems designed and constructed in accordance with a current standard. Where an existing tank has been provided in accordance with a different standard, the systems should be assessed according to the requirements of those original standards. In particular, if the vessel's safe working pressure is less than 12 bar gauge (174 psig), then the air system pressure, relief devices etc all have to be altered to suit, and the delivery system has to be arranged so as to be capable of working within the storage tank conditions. It is recommended that such tanks are replaced with tanks meeting the requirements of paragraph 88. The timing of the replacement should be agreed with your chlorine supplier and the competent person who examines your vessels.

Connecting pipework and means for isolation of storage tanks

90 The main connections to the storage tanks are:

(a) liquid chlorine inlet;

(b) liquid chlorine outlet;

(c) vent lines and compressed dry gas lines;

(d) relief system;

(e) instrumentation and pressure gauges.

Connections at the top of the chlorine storage tank. Note the pressures relief system with interlocked valves (see paragraphs 120 to 127)

91 You need to keep the number of connections to a minimum to reduce the potential sources of leakage. The arrangements of valves and pipework should be made as simple as possible to minimise errors in operation. Pipework isolation valves should be fitted directly to the branches on the manlid or the tank itself. The system should be designed and operated so that, if the joints between the valves and the storage tanks fail, gaseous chlorine only will be released (see paragraphs 94-96).

Safety advice for bulk chlorine installations

92   Whenever two valves are installed in series for isolation, it is recommended that the system of operation is planned so that each valve is used exclusively for a defined period during normal operation. This ensures that both valves are kept in operable condition at all times.

93   An application of the principles in this section is shown diagrammatically in Figure 2. Not all installations will be to this pattern, and variations (some of which are described in the text) may be appropriate.

Liquid chlorine inlet

94   The liquid chlorine inlet should not normally extend further into the tank than the maximum liquid level. Some older installations use a dip-pipe on the inlet line. To avoid liquid chlorine flowing back if the filling line fails, holes are drilled in the top of the dip-pipe so that liquid will not siphon back. A full dip-pipe may be provided as an inlet to a vessel used for both importation and exportation. Such vessels need to be fitted with the additional controls appropriate to a liquid chlorine outlet. You should discuss the controls needed with your proposed chlorine supplier at an early stage.

95   The isolation valve on the chlorine inlet line, directly bolted to the flange on the storage tank, should preferably be a billet or high integrity globe valve. A back-up valve should be provided, which may be remotely operated. If a manual back-up valve is used, the isolation valve at the delivery point end of the pipework should be remotely operable from the emergency stop points.

Liquid chlorine outlet

96   The removal of liquid chlorine from the storage tank is by means of a dip-pipe. You therefore need to make arrangements to prevent chlorine releases caused by the joint between the isolation valve and storage tank failing. This is most satisfactorily achieved on new plant by use of a billet-type globe valve, bolted to the flanged branch on the storage tank, with the dip-pipe screwed into the bottom of the valve.

97   You need to back up the main isolation valve with an additional valve to enable isolation if one valve fails to seat effectively. Depending on the local piping arrangement, provision of one or more remotely controlled valves is recommended for emergency control. A remotely operated valve which is designed to give positive isolation and which is suitably positioned may also serve as one of the two isolation valves required.

98   In addition, it is strongly recommended that you incorporate a restricting orifice in the line to the consuming plant. The object of this is to reduce the size of a release from a major failure to as low as reasonably practicable, ie appreciably less than the full-bore flow through the pipe. The size and location of the orifice needs careful consideration. The orifice should not be so small as to lead to problems, such as proneness of the orifice to blocking, etc. In some cases it may be practicable to limit the flow in the line to the maximum required by the process. The orifice should not be located within the dip-pipe because of the problem of removing the liquid chlorine from the tank in the event of a blockage of the orifice. In some

DESIGN AND LOCATION OF INSTALLATIONS

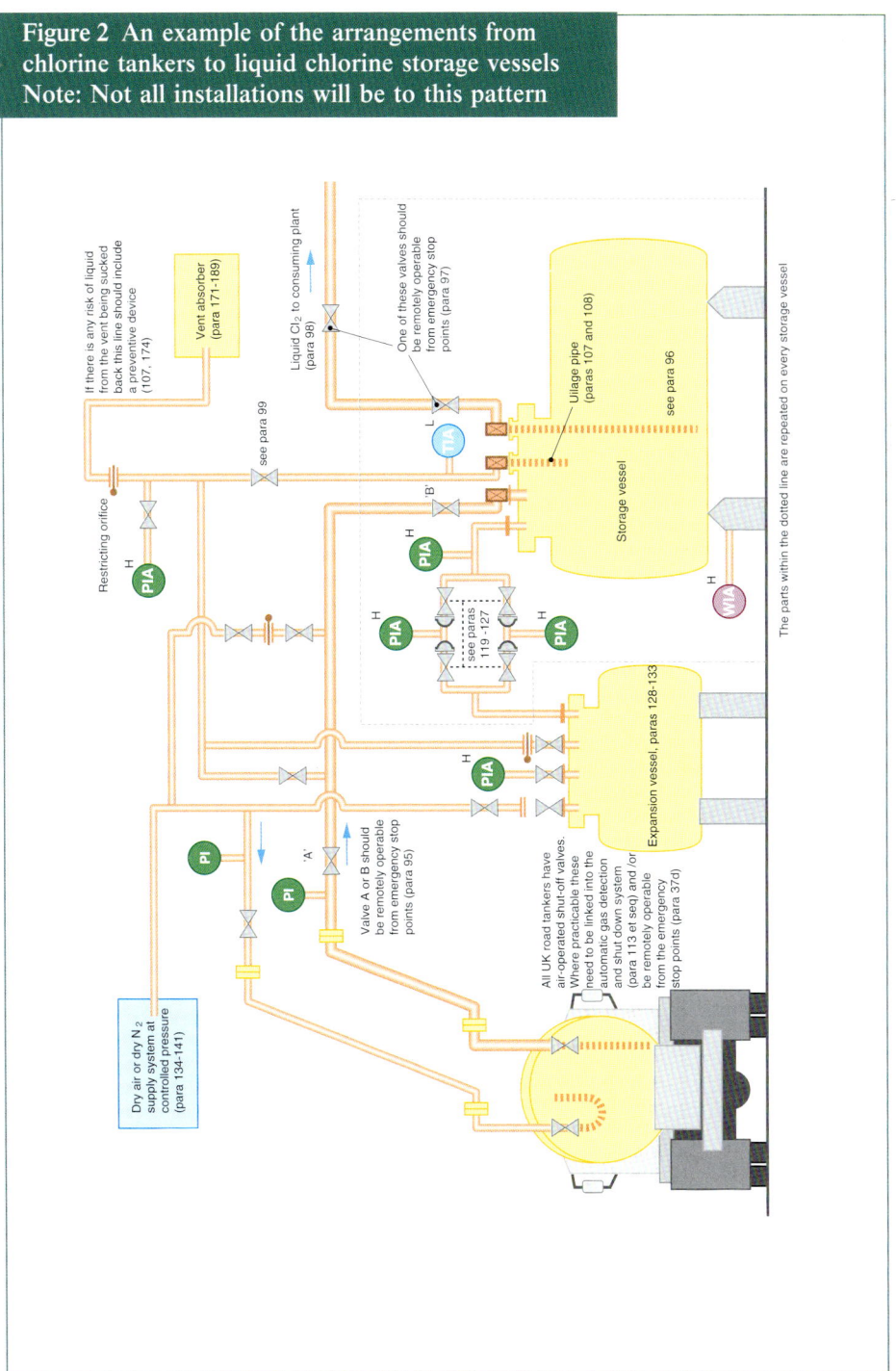

Figure 2 An example of the arrangements from chlorine tankers to liquid chlorine storage vessels
Note: Not all installations will be to this pattern

plants, the flow restriction can be replaced by the remotely operable shut-off valves (see paragraph 111) controlled by a suitable flow or pressure sensor. Excess flow valves may be advisable for lines normally taking a flow of chlorine much less than the flow which could pass through in fault conditions. They are not suitable for lines in which the normal flow rate is high, and for which other means of fault detection and flow isolation should be used.

Vent and compressed dry gas lines

99   Vent lines and compressed dry gas lines can be connected to the storage tank either through separate inlets or through a combined single inlet. In either case, the valve directly connected to the storage tank should be backed up by a second valve.

100   The prevention of suck-back of aqueous liquor into the vent line requires similar precautions to those described for vaporisers (see paragraph 161). The prevention of back-diffusion of moisture is described in paragraphs 178-181. The inlet to the scrubbing system should include a lute pipe (barometric leg) to prevent liquid from the scrubbing system entering the chlorine system.

101   The procedure for transferring liquid chlorine to the storage tanks should provide for the vent valve to be opened slightly at the end of discharge for about a minute (see Appendix 6, paragraph 17) to confirm that the tank has not been significantly over-filled, ie above the extra-high level alarm (see paragraph 104). Overfilling is indicated by frosting on the vent line, in which case pressure relief may be necessary (see paragraphs 102-132).

Relief system

102   The special requirements for the isolation valves on the pressure relief system on the storage tanks are covered in paragraphs 123-133.

Instrumentation and chlorine detector systems

103   Control instrumentation on storage tanks and elsewhere in the installation should, wherever possible, be designed to fail safe. Electrical and electronic equipment, unless specially protected against corrosion, should not be placed in areas where it could be affected by gas leaks.

104   Storage tank contents. The quantity of liquid chlorine in each storage tank is preferably determined by installing the tank on load cells or on a weighbridge. Load cells should be recalibrated whenever the vessel is inspected and pressure-tested with water. Accuracy checks can also be made against the weight of chlorine supplied whenever a delivery is made, provided the plant is off-line. It is recommended that load cells are recalibrated at intervals not exceeding three years. The weight of liquid chlorine in each tank should be indicated locally and may be repeated in the plant control room. The contents-measuring devices need to operate a high-contents alarm in the control room (and on complex plants, possibly an extra-high contents alarm) for safety reasons. The extra-high level alarm needs to be run independently of the system giving the high-contents alarm, for reliability reasons. When fitted, it is recommended that the extra-high level alarm is used to automatically close the tank inlet valve and the tanker outlet valve, see paragraph 105.

DESIGN AND LOCATION OF INSTALLATIONS

105 As an alternative to the measurement of the quantity of liquid chlorine by weight, measurement by liquid level in the tanks is also acceptable. However, selection of suitable equipment is difficult and you should discuss it with your chlorine supplier. Such devices are preferred as the means of triggering the extra-high level alarm.

106 To limit the liquid volume in the storage tank to that permitted by the filling ratio (see paragraph 88(c)), an ullage pipe can be screwed into the bottom of the valve on the vent line. The length of this ullage pipe needs to be consistent with the filling ratio so that, if liquid chlorine rises above the correct level, it will flow through the ullage pipe when the vent valve is opened at the end of a delivery (see Appendix 6) or in response to an alarm. The ullage pipe should be checked when the routine inspection of the storage installation is made. A low temperature or other alarm (see paragraph 107) should be fitted on the vent line from the storage tanks to warn if liquid chlorine is entering the ullage pipe on the vent line.

107 On a simple installation, with good staffing and attendance at the tanks, an ullage pipe (see paragraph 106) may serve as the extra-high level alarm. You need to be aware that this method requires the vent line to be left open, which is not necessarily the case for alternative methods, see Appendix 6. If a high contents alarm is ignored during filling of the tank, the liquid reaches the bottom of the ullage pipe and evaporates in the vent-line above the vent control valve, producing frosting of the pipe. An ullage pipe therefore presents the risk of liquid chlorine being passed to the scrubber unless the line contains a knock-out device fitted with a high level alarm. A knock-out pot in the vent line with level alarms is also recommended for other reasons (see paragraph 157). The minimum protection fitted should be a restriction orifice plate (see paragraph 98) and a low temperature alarm.

108 Ullage pipes are not recommended for contents indication on new installations; instead an extra-high level alarm on the tank should be installed, see also paragraph 105.

109 A low contents alarm may be useful for operational reasons and may have safety implications if, eg there could be process upsets on failure of chlorine supply or passage of padding air (see paragraph 226) into a downstream vessel.

110 Storage tank pressure. The pressure in the chlorine storage tanks is usually measured by gauges specially developed for use with liquid chlorine; these have silver or tantalum diaphragms. Before use, the gauges need to be completely degreased (eg with steam and/or a detergent), dried and all traces of solvent removed, and be pressure-tested using only clean, dry, oil-free compressed air. The pressure gauges may be fitted with switches to give an alarm if the pressure exceeds, or falls below, a pre-set value. Alternatively, pressure switches may be used to give an independent signal for the high and low pressure alarms.

111 Where reference is made to flow or pressure sensors 'operating' valves (see paragraph 98) there is a choice whether the operation is automatic or via manual intervention (see paragraph 62(b)). At the extremes, operation should be automatic

in an unstaffed plant, and may be indirect in a well-instrumented plant with a continuously staffed control room.

112   Equipment associated with the automatic pressure relief system is described in paragraphs 120 and 128-133.

Chlorine detectors and alarms

113   The air in a building housing chlorine storage tanks should be continuously monitored using proprietary chlorine detector systems to give warning of chlorine leakage. Detectors are strongly recommended in buildings which are not continuously staffed to provide early warning of leaks, allowing prompt remedial action. For outdoor installations, the value of detector systems needs to be assessed by considering factors such as the size of the installation, the staffing levels and the response times achievable. On detecting a leak, the detector should:

(a)   raise an audible alarm in a continuously staffed area or control centre;

(b)   activate audible alarms in the affected area;

(c)   operate the automatic isolation valves; and

(d)   control the mechanical ventilation, if fitted.

114   Audible alarms need to have a distinct tone. In addition, warning lights of the amber flashing or traffic light type may be fitted outside each chlorine building. Where appropriate, eg at large, remote or sensitive sites, alarms should be connected to a telemetry system to provide warning at a staffed control point. The control point should be able to isolate the chlorine supply, preferably via a remotely operable valve fitted to the outlet of the tank.

115   Chlorine detectors may be placed in storage and plant areas. The manufacturer or supplier of the system should advise on the best location for the sensors; typically sensors are mounted between 0.3 m and 0.5 m above ground level, and at the outlet from fume scrubbers. For indoor installations, sensors may need to be located in or near the entrance to ducts carrying chlorine pipework, and the air intakes to extractor fans. Where forced ventilation systems have been installed, the detector should be located at the outlet of the system; where this is not reasonably practicable the detector should be placed near the storage and use areas.

116   Detection systems should provide a continuous monitoring function when chlorine is in storage or in use. Chlorine gas sensors should be tested regularly in accordance with the manufacturer's instructions to demonstrate that the detector and its associated circuits are functioning correctly. A record of such tests is recommended. The detection system should operate the alarm circuits in the event of power loss, sensor failure, or low condition of the standby batteries. All alarm relay operations should be protected by a battery back-up facility.

117   The detector system should activate the low level alarm at a chlorine concentration of 1-5 ppm. Lower settings are liable to activate the system at every tank-filling operation, unless

a duration requirement is also imposed. For example, some companies set the low level alarm at 0.5 ppm, but require the sensor to register this concentration for at least 30 seconds, to avoid spurious trips of the alarm system during filling operations. For indoor installations, the low alarm level should activate the ventilation fan, open the intake louvers, and activate local audio alarms and any remote telemetry alarm.

118   Multi-stage detector systems are sometimes used to give an indication of the severity of the malfunction to personnel outside a chlorine room. It is suggested that the high level alarm operates at about three times the level of the first-stage alarm, ie 3-15 ppm, depending on the duration that the sensor needs to register this level. However, some companies set the high level alarm at 2 ppm with a 30 second duration requirement.

On activation of a high level alarm the ventilation system should be shut off, the auto-shut down system activated (where fitted) and the high level alarm sounded. The tone of the alarm at low and high levels should be different and operators trained to recognise the difference and how to respond in each case. Local alarms may be supplemented by telemetry links to control rooms, where appropriate. The response to alarms is covered in paragraphs 247-263. Some sensors can be damaged by high chlorine concentrations; detector systems should therefore be checked after any high level alarm.

PROTECTION OF STORAGE VESSELS AGAINST OVERPRESSURE

119   High pressure on the liquid chlorine storage tank is indicated by a high pressure alarm (paragraph 110). Overpressure in the liquid chlorine storage tanks can result from over-filling or excessive padding pressure. Over-filling with liquid chlorine is indicated by alarms on the weigh system used to determine the liquid chlorine content of the storage tanks (paragraphs 104-109). Overpressure on the compressed air or nitrogen supply to the storage tank is prevented by the installation of a relief valve on the supply source of the compressed gas. The supply source should be well upstream of the tank and separated from it by isolation valves (paragraph 139).

Relief system

120   The storage tanks need to be protected against overpressure by a suitable automatic pressure relief system which is set to operate at a pressure below the design value. The preferred pressure relief system consists of two bursting discs placed back to back. A bursting disc followed by a relief valve may also be used, but is always subject to the risk of corrosion of the relief valve. Protection of the relief valve from corrosion must be carefully considered if the bursting disc relief valve system is used. The use of relief valves alone is not recommended because of the corrosion or blockage which could occur if a relief valve were left continuously exposed to chlorine. Whichever system is used, you should provide a pressure alarm/indicator between the two discs or between the disc and relief valve (see paragraph 133). In the latter arrangement it is good practice to remove and overhaul the relief valve whenever the bursting disc is replaced.

121   The discharge line from the pressure relief system normally enters a closed expansion vessel (except in a few specialised arrangements). Any pressure in the expansion vessel or between components in the relief system reduces the protection given to the storage vessel (see paragraphs 85, 128-133). Special relief arrangements are usually required when there is a significant risk of overpressure from continuous pressure sources such as radiant heat or by pumping chlorine. Under these circumstances relief into a closed expansion vessel may be inadequate. Relief arrangements based on relief valves into an 'open' system (eg a vent scrubber) may be preferable to bursting discs, as the valves reseat once the source of overpressure has been removed. This arrangement is normally only found on larger installations; you should consult your chlorine supplier.

Bursting discs

122   Bursting discs (which are designed to fail at or below the design pressure of storage tanks) are commonly made of nickel, although tantalum, silver or other compatible materials may be used. Uncoated graphite is not recommended. Discs should comply with BS 2915[49] (or equivalent standard) and should be carefully selected for the operating temperature range, as the rupture pressure is temperature-dependent.

Arrangements for relief systems

123   On simple installations, such as those with a single storage vessel and associated expansion vessel, a single bursting disc system without any isolating valves, installed directly on the storage vessel, may be acceptable. In practice, however, it is more convenient to install a valved system to allow replacement of discs under a controlled system of work, without needing to completely empty and purge the system. Where two or more storage vessels share an expansion vessel, the relief arrangements should allow prompt replacement of discs and venting of all excess pressure out of the expansion vessel.

124   The preferred arrangements are shown in Figures 3 and 4 and should be used on all new installations. The isolating valves may be mechanically interlocked (recommended for new installations) so that one pair of discs is always operative, or the isolating valves may be individually locked. To be effective the bursting discs need to be of the simple domed unsupported type with the concave side facing in the directions shown in Figures 3, 4, and 5. The identifying tags should be left attached to each disc so that they can be identified as having been installed correctly. Existing older installations using the arrangement shown in Figure 5 should replace it with a preferred arrangement (Figure 3 or 4) when major modifications are in hand.

125   The valves which remain open must permit the operational devices to discharge at the required rate to an expansion vessel. Pipework before the isolating valves should be as short and simple as possible to minimise the risk of chlorine leakage from joints and pipework; the isolation using valves before the bursting discs should preferably be fitted directly on flanged connections on the manlid of the storage tanks.

DESIGN AND LOCATION OF INSTALLATIONS

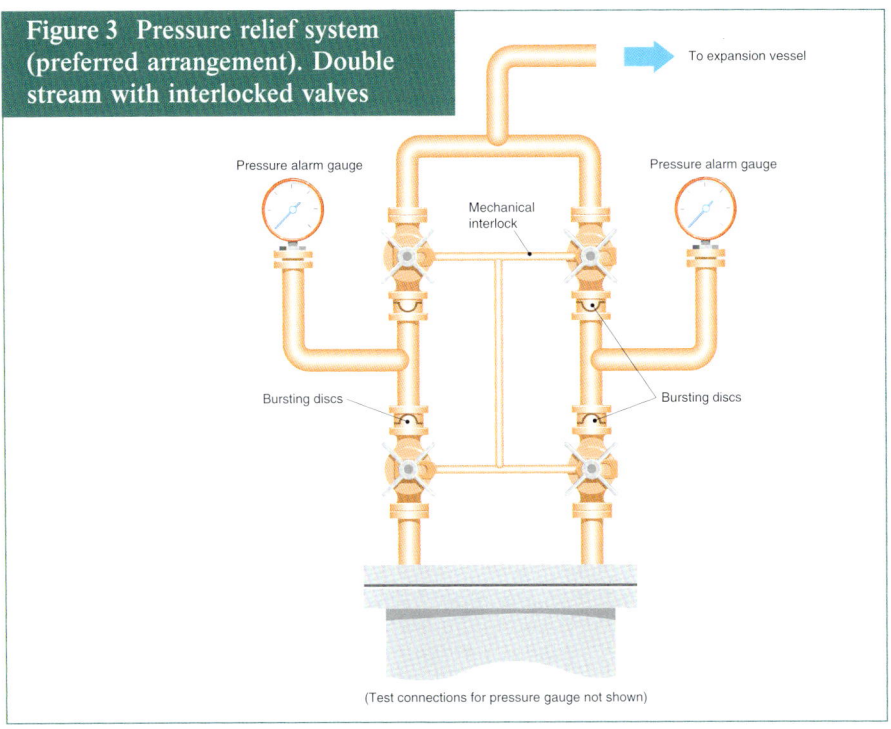

Figure 3 Pressure relief system (preferred arrangement). Double stream with interlocked valves

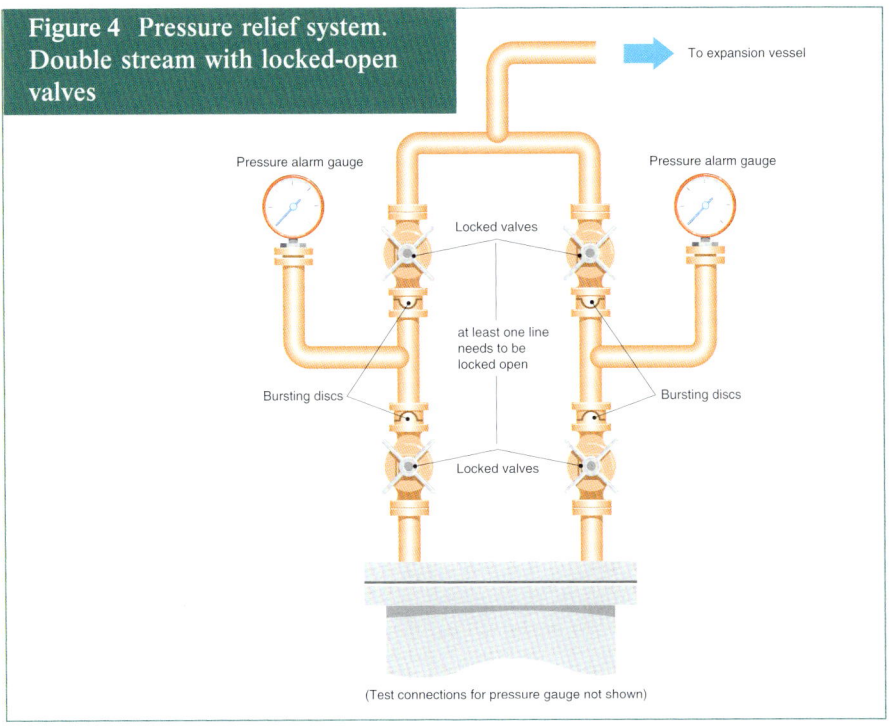

Figure 4 Pressure relief system. Double stream with locked-open valves

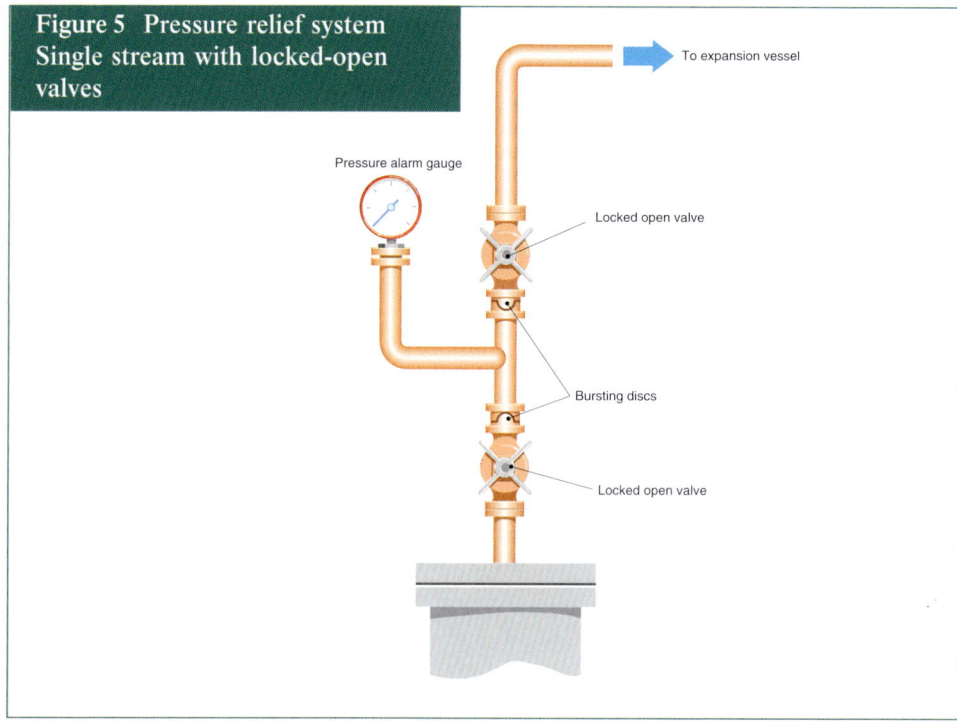

Figure 5 Pressure relief system Single stream with locked-open valves

126   Your procedures for dealing with a failure of a bursting disc should be clearly defined. Base them on the principle that at no time should pressures beyond the design range be allowed to develop (see also paragraph 127).

127   At any installation where a 'locked'-open isolating valve precedes a bursting disc, a safe system of work should be defined to prevent unacceptable pressures from any source occurring in the vessel while the isolating valve is closed. The procedures need to cover the safe removal of the vessel from normal service, stabilising the pressure, changing the bursting disc, venting the expansion tank and returning the vessel to normal use. Such safe systems will vary with plant design but should:

(a)   be in a written form, unambiguous and readily available;

(b)   include a permit-to-work system;

(c)   be included in plant personnel training programmes;

(d)   be properly supervised with responsibilities clearly allocated;

(e)   be regularly updated and periodically subjected to HAZOP [50] review, particularly when plant design, operating procedures or management systems are modified; and

(f)   be rigidly adhered to.

Expansion vessels

Expansion vessel mounted in a bund

128   The design requirements for the construction of the expansion vessel are similar to those for the storage tanks; the capacity of the expansion vessel should be at least 10% of the largest storage vessel.

129   The expansion vessel should be capable of being vented manually to an absorption system; the vent valve is normally locked closed. Controlled venting should be through a suitable flow restriction device, eg an orifice plate to prevent overload of the absorption system.

130   The expansion vessel should be provided with a pressure-sensing device which gives an alarm if pressure builds up in the vessel. The alarm system needs to be capable of being tested regularly to ensure that it is operable (see paragraph 133).

131   Arrange the compressed air or nitrogen connection to the expansion vessel to avoid the possibility of inadvertently pressurising the vessel. This may be achieved by physical disconnection, isolating blanking plates, or by double block valves supported by a safe system of work. If an expansion vessel serves more than one storage vessel, make arrangements for prompt response to a pressure alarm signal from it.

132   While the risk of the expansion vessel itself being over-pressurised with chlorine is minimal because of the precautions described in paragraphs 128-131, you should establish procedural or mechanical means to ensure that this cannot occur.

Pressure alarms

133   There should be a high-pressure alarm on every storage vessel, and an additional pressure indicator/alarm at each important safety location on the relief arrangement. This means that one additional pressure alarm may suffice on each storage vessel that has its own expansion vessel, and that alarm may be either in the relief line (if there is a single bursting disc) or on the expansion vessel. When one expansion vessel serves several storage vessels, there should be an additional pressure alarm within each relief assembly and also one on the expansion vessel. Test alarms regularly (at least monthly) by gas injection or moving contacts.

ARRANGEMENTS FOR UNLOADING OF LIQUID CHLORINE FROM ROAD TANKERS TO STORAGE

Unloading Using Dry Compressed Air or Dry Nitrogen

Air compressor unit

134 The recommended system for transferring liquid chlorine from chlorine tankers to storage vessels, by 'padding' with dry air or dry nitrogen, is outlined in Figure 2 and in Appendix 6 which provides a sound basis for developing local procedures. Detailed requirements, which supplement information given in previous sections, are reviewed in paragraphs 135-147. You need to agree your arrangements with your supplier and design them to minimise the risk of overpressure.

135 A separate and independent dry compressed air or nitrogen system should be used for chlorine duty, to minimise the possibility of back-diffusion of chlorine which could lead to dangerous conditions in other air-consuming units, particularly instrumentation. Compressed nitrogen may be produced in a liquid nitrogen evaporation unit.

136 If you use compressed air, your supply needs to be oil-free and have a dew point below -40°C. Normally, air should be compressed to around 10 bar gauge using a truly oil-free compressor (1.5 m^3/min free air capacity); if an oil-lubricated compressor is used it must be fitted with an oil filter which must be regularly maintained.

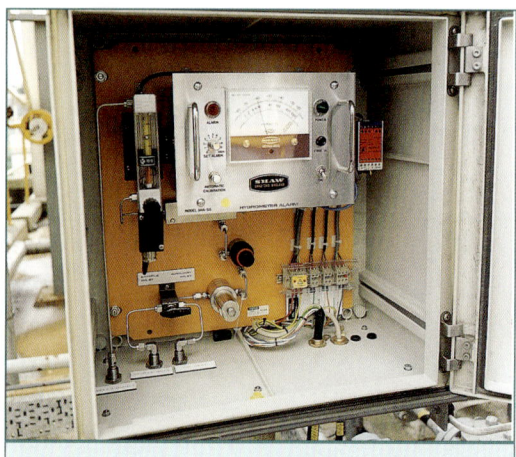

Hygrometer alarm. At this installation the compressed air dew point is less than - 60°C

137 The compressed air is cooled to remove part of the moisture content and finally dried, using a regenerative-type drying system, to a dew point below -40°C. The dew point should preferably be monitored continuously using a monitor provided with an alarm that gives warning if the dew point exceeds a pre-set figure. It is important to recharge or regenerate drying agents according to the equipment and chlorine suppliers' advice.

138 A guard tower, filled with anhydrous calcium chloride or other suitable material, may be installed after the regenerative system as a further safeguard. For small installations a

drier alone using anhydrous calcium chloride or other drying agent may be adequate, provided that proper checks on the condition of the drying agent are made.

Supply of dry padding gas to the system

139 The compressed dry air or dry nitrogen should be stored in a pressure receiver. This should be fitted with a relief valve set to operate at the chlorine storage plant's safe working pressure or 10 bar gauge, whichever is lower. From the receiver the gas should pass through a non-return valve, or a pressure-actuated shut-off valve, followed by a reducing valve to give a supply at the pressure required for unloading the tankers. This supply will also be suitable for other purposes on the chlorine plant, such as drying out or purging of pipelines and vessels provided precautions are taken to prevent backflow of chlorine into the air system. Pressure gauges should be installed upstream and downstream of the pressure reducing valve so that checks can be made that the padding gas pressure is greater than the chlorine pressure. It is important to provide safeguards [23-25] to ensure that excessive gas pressures cannot be applied to the chlorine system. This may be particularly important if the padding gas is supplied from high pressure cylinders.

140 The liquid chlorine discharge line on the chlorine tanker should be connected to the permanent pipework at the unloading point (see paragraphs 43-55). The pipework connecting the unloading point to the liquid chlorine storage vessels should be reasonably short (see also paragraphs (53-60). If it is necessary to use a long liquid chlorine line to storage, you must consider the need to protect this line against overpressure (see paragraphs 61-67).

141 A pressure gauge, a vent line to the absorber and a connection for dry compressed gas should be installed close to the end of the permanent pipework at the unloading point, with the necessary isolation valves, as detailed in Figure 2.

Unloading using chlorine gas pressure

142 Liquid chlorine may be transferred from the chlorine tankers to the storage vessels by padding with dry chlorine gas. The gas is normally taken from one of the stock tanks but this should preferably not be the one into which the tanker is being unloaded. The supply of dry chlorine gas at the required pressure may be obtained by re-compressing chlorine vapour from a storage tank or by vaporisation of liquid chlorine. A source of dry, compressed, oil-free air or nitrogen is still required, for drying out and purging the system.

Use of re-compressed chlorine vapour

143 Selection of the appropriate compressor for re-compression of chlorine vapour requires careful consideration to ensure that the equipment can operate satisfactorily on an intermittent basis. Diaphragm compressors or dry carbon ring reciprocating compressors are suitable for this duty provided that maintenance is carried out on a regular basis.

144 Diaphragm compressors should use stainless steel double diaphragms with inert fluid between them. Dry carbon ring compressors should preferably be purged with dry air after use, to avoid problems resulting from residual chlorine in the compressor leaking from shaft glands. During operation of the compressor, the shaft glands should be pressurised with dry, compressed, inert gas.

145 If cooling of the compressor body is required, this should preferably be accomplished by air cooling. If jacket cooling is necessary, this should be achieved by circulation through an external heat exchanger with provision to detect leakage of chlorine into the heat exchange fluid. Direct water cooling should be avoided.

146 The compressor needs to be fitted with a bypass so that the chlorine can be recycled until its temperature is raised sufficiently to prevent liquefaction in the delivery lines. The temperature of the chlorine should be monitored using an indicator which is fitted with an alarm, set to sound if it exceeds 90°C.

147 A pressure relief system on the compressor delivery line should also be provided to prevent the delivery pressure exceeding a pre-set figure (see paragraph 139).

CHLORINE VAPORISERS

148 Vaporisers (also known as evaporators) convert liquid chlorine into gas. A major use of chlorine vaporisers is in water treatment, to control weed and algae in cooling water and to sterilise drinking water. These units are frequently supplied as part of a package with other dosing or analytical equipment. Vaporisers are always required with a fixed or demountable bulk tank, to obtain a regular, steady supply of gas to process. The drawing of gas from the vapour space of a bulk tank is unsatisfactory and unsafe. There is the risk of process liquids passing back into the tank, irregularity of supply and the possible accumulation of less volatile, dangerous impurities, such as explosive nitrogen trichloride in the tank.[51] The safe handling of chlorine containing nitrogen trichloride is discussed elsewhere.[52]

Types

149 There are four main types of vaporiser (see also Appendix 7):

(a) Vertical tube bundle. These resemble ordinary heat exchangers, usually with the chlorine in the tubes. Alternative formats include the common vaporiser used in water treatment (a cylinder with a dip-pipe liquid chlorine inlet immersed in the heating bath) or a shell and tube heat exchanger with the chlorine on the shell side. A bayonet vaporiser is very similar.

(b) Coil. The chlorine is evaporated in a coil of steel tubing running inside a wet steam bath or a water bath heated by steam or electricity.

(c) Concentric tube. The heat exchange surface is a tube, typically four inches in diameter, surrounded by a heating jacket.

DESIGN AND LOCATION OF INSTALLATIONS

Coil in bath vaporiser heated by low pressure steam

(d) Kettle. Kettle evaporators are used on large capacity systems. They contain a heater system (usually a tube bundle of hot water or heated fluid - not steam) passing through a vessel containing liquid chlorine. Kettle evaporators do not superheat the chlorine vapour, other systems do.

Regulation of throughput

Self-regulating vaporisers

150   In some types of vaporiser the liquid chlorine is fed in at the bottom and gas is drawn off via a control valve at the top. When demand is high, the liquid chlorine level rises in the container, and a greater heat exchange surface area is presented to the liquid. When demand is low, the greater vapour pressure at the temperature of the heating medium drives the liquid chlorine out of the vaporiser back into the storage vessel and the evaporation rate falls. This system is usually applicable to vaporisers with a relatively small chlorine capacity, ie vertical tube bundles, coil types and concentric tube types. Bayonet vaporisers can be used for high vaporisation rates. On water treatment plants a self-regulating vaporiser, with an electrically heated water bath is usually used.

Constant level vaporisers

151   Other types of vaporisers, usually found only in large-capacity plants, sacrifice certain advantages of the self-regulating types to achieve much larger vaporisation rates. These vaporisers require separate instrumentation and control arrangements to provide a constant level of liquid chlorine in the kettle or shell with high and low level alarms. In such types (where there can be parts of the liquid chlorine pool which are not well-mixed), there is a greater tendency to concentrate the less volatile impurities than in a self-regulating vaporiser. A separate purge and vaporiser circuit may be required to deal periodically with the residues. The design and operation of these larger-capacity vaporisers is a specialised topic, and requires consultation between the user, the designer, and the chlorine supplier as the risk of nitrogen trichloride enrichment and subsequent explosion is increased.[51, 52] You should involve your supplier when assessing this risk.

Methods of heating

152   The methods of heating the vaporiser should minimise both the risk of corrosion and vaporiser failure. These include: heating with hot water; heating with low pressure steam; and using closed circuit heating with heat transfer fluids other than water. Direct electrical heating should not be used because of the risk of local overheating and chlorine/iron fires (see paragraph 158 and Appendix 2).

(a) Heating with hot water. This is the most frequently used method; the normal working temperature (60-70°C) is well below that at which any significant reaction of carbon steel occurs with dry chlorine.

(b) Heating with steam. The steam should be saturated and its pressure should be limited to less than 1 bar gauge to avoid overheating, particularly if the vaporiser is made of mild steel. Any small leaks of chlorine to the water side of hot water or steam types lead to very rapid corrosion of the steel by moist chlorine (see paragraph 169). Steam systems must meet the requirements of the PSTGC Regulations.[23-25] The greater flexibility of steam heating is useful on plants using chlorine gas at high or at very variable rates.

(c) Heat transfer fluids (other than water). Electrical or steam heat can be applied to a heat transfer fluid which is relatively unreactive towards chlorine. The available fluids (eg hexachlorobutadiene) are themselves hazardous, so that the hazards of using water as heat transfer medium are in practice accepted, with suitable safeguards.

General installation

153 The vaporiser should be installed in the storage area or in an adjacent space as close as possible to the chlorine storage tanks in order to keep pipelines carrying liquid chlorine short. Long pipe runs will require pressure relief (see paragraphs 61-67). Changeover of liquid chlorine supply from one storage tank to another can affect operating conditions in the vaporiser system and any such difficulties will be reduced if the spacing is not too great, eg less than 5 metres. Nevertheless, the space between the vaporiser and the storage system should be such as to allow adequate access for emergency action in the event of an incident at the vaporiser.

Hazards

154 The quantity of chlorine in a chlorine vaporiser system is relatively small compared with that normally contained in the main chlorine storage tanks. Nevertheless, the system design should be such that failure of equipment can be detected and rectified quickly and that any consequent release of chlorine to the environment is minimised.

155 Potential hazards associated with chlorine vaporisers include:

(a) Pinhole leaks leading to rapid corrosion and increased loss of chlorine.

(b) Rapid corrosion, if any moisture is allowed into the chlorine system.

(c) Possible concentration of impurities in the chlorine as it is evaporated, such as explosive nitrogen trichloride. This needs to be discussed with your chlorine supplier.

(d) Reverse flow of reaction fluids, caused by a fall in pressure in the vaporiser, or by excess pressure in the process, or by solution of chlorine gas in the fluid. The presence of the fluid (water, solvent or reagent) in the vaporiser can cause corrosion or local violent reaction leading to rapid overpressure and possible rupture of the vaporiser.

(e) Carry-over of liquid chlorine as bulk fluid or droplets into the gas line or into the process itself. This can (depending on the materials of construction and on the process) cause damage or hazard.

(f) Excessive gas pressure to the system due to overheating a vaporiser, since the vapour pressure of chlorine rises very steeply with temperature
(see Appendix 2, Figure A2.1).

(g) Excessive hydraulic forces, if the system is closed up and full of liquid due to the expansion of liquid chlorine when heated.

These basic hazards are considered in more detail in paragraphs 156-161, but grouped according to the type of hazard.

Flooding and liquid carry-over

156 Flooding (filling) of the chlorine vaporiser with liquid chlorine may result from operation of the equipment above its capacity, inadequate heating, or fouling of the heat transfer surfaces. The temperature of the heating medium is usually controlled thermostatically. If the temperature of the heating medium falls too low in a self-regulating evaporator, it is possible for the outgoing gas to be inadequately superheated, or for flooding to occur. Flooding results in carry-over of liquid chlorine into the vapour lines, and a potential hazard (depending on the process and plant materials). The same may happen if the level of water in a water bath falls. In the extreme, if chlorine is drawn off but no heat is supplied to the vaporiser, it is possible for ice to form on the heat exchanger surfaces and damage them severely. You should consider installing a gas flow rate indicator. This may be of value to the operator for routine purposes, and will also indicate excessive withdrawal rates.

157 You should consider fitting a knockout pot (or spray catcher) to prevent chlorine droplets and spray from passing into gas pipework when liquid chlorine might damage the material of the pipes, or cause the process to become unstable. In all cases where the possibility of liquid passing to process is unacceptable, it is strongly recommended that a low temperature alarm be fitted near the knockout pot and arranged to cut off the liquid chlorine supply to the vaporiser or (in self-regulating types only) the gaseous chlorine outlet may be closed, driving the liquid chlorine back into the storage vessel(s). Adequate instrumentation and alarms should always be provided to give immediate warning of this condition. High and low bath temperature and level alarms with shut-down facilities are recommended.

Accelerated corrosion and reaction (high temperature)

158 To avoid rapid corrosion of the water side of heat exchange surfaces made from galvanised steel, operating temperatures should not exceed $70^{\circ}C$. If operation at higher temperatures is required, vaporisers made of nickel or nickel alloys (such as Monel 400 or Inconel) should be used. In such cases, the downstream chlorine

gas pipework may also need upgrading to ensure adequate resistance to corrosion at elevated temperatures.

159 If the heating medium is steam, the temperature can be monitored by low pressure and high pressure alarms on the steam inlet. The pressure of steam should normally be limited to 1 bar gauge (120°C equivalent) and the steam has to be saturated, not superheated.

High pressure

160 Precautions must [23] be in place to protect the system against over-pressurisation, eg a pressure relief device. Pressure relief devices and high pressure alarms, where fitted, should be properly designed and installed, maintained in an effective working order, and tested regularly. They must be periodically examined by a competent person.[53] A typical working temperature for a vaporiser is 70°C. The vapour pressure of chlorine at 70°C exceeds 21 bar, (see Figure A2.1, Appendix 2). It follows that you need to take the following steps to:

(a) Ensure that the vaporiser is not isolated when full of liquid chlorine. Strict observance of written procedures for shut-down is vital.

(b) Avoid accidentally isolating the vaporiser on both sides. Care needs to be taken to ensure that the closing arrangements for the emergency valves take this into account (see paragraphs 162-165).

(c) Design the vaporiser shell and pipes to withstand the working pressure and duty.

(d) Implement operational controls which minimise the risk of the working pressure being exceeded.

If your chlorine vaporiser is not supplied with a pressure relief device you will need to adopt procedures, or fit suitable pressure relief, to ensure that the conditions in (a) to (d) are met.

Reverse flow

161 You should eliminate the possibility of suck-back into the vaporisers by suitable design. For example, water chlorinating package systems usually incorporate a set of valves in the control system to prevent suck-back or push-back. The arrangements vary, and care needs to be taken to ensure that the system provided does give protection in the event of, eg, a leak at the ejector non-return valve. You should also consider fitting a low pressure gas alarm to the outlet gas line. This gives warning of loss of supply to the process, and may indicate a need to start purging the system, using dry air or other suitable dry gas (dew point less than -40°C) to prevent suck-back. Whatever method is used, the system needs to be regularly inspected and maintained, and adequate records kept.

DESIGN AND LOCATION OF INSTALLATIONS

Routine and emergency isolation

162 The vaporiser has to be capable of being isolated for maintenance, or in an emergency, such as a failure of the vaporiser itself through leakage or a failure of the gas line downstream. In addition to a manual valve on the liquid inlet and on the gas outlet, remotely or automatically operable valves are strongly recommended on both inlet and outlet. A pressure-reducing or flow control valve will almost always be fitted on the outlet and it is sometimes possible for this valve to be the remotely operable shut-off valve.

163 Your risk assessment should consider the need for additional protection in the event that automatic valves fail to operate (or remotely operable valves are not activated) in an emergency. For example a flow restriction in the liquid inlet (typically on the exit from the storage tank(s)), will limit the release which could occur in the event of a major plant failure.

Emergency shutdown push button at the vaporiser. Also shown in one of six chlorine detectors at this installation which can also automatically shut down the chlorine installation (see paragraphs 113-118)

164 The hazards of totally isolating the vaporiser are considerable and will be most severe when the evaporator is full (eg if the valves close together in a condition of major gas line failure). If there is a gas space above the liquid chlorine when the vaporiser is isolated and heated, the internal pressure will reach that of chlorine at the heating medium temperature. The vaporiser, lines and valves need to be designed to withstand such pressure or incorporate arrangements to relieve to a safe place. The control of automatic valves needs to be arranged so that the valves do not close together when an alarm is raised (see also paragraph 160). One approach is to arrange for the gas control valve to close on alarms related to improper working of the system (eg low gas pressure, downstream process alarms, low temperature) and the liquid control valve at the storage tank to close on chlorine release (eg detectors local to the vaporiser and storage, or manual alarms). If the plant is continually staffed, manual intervention may be a suitable alternative to providing wholly automatic operation of shut-down. However, procedures need to be established to ensure that this does not introduce significant delays into the response to an alarm. An alternative approach is to use a pressure control globe valve for remote isolation of the outlet line so that excessive pressures will lift it slightly off its seat, preventing excessive overpressures. Relief pressures and valve direction need careful consideration and should be discussed with the valve supplier.

165 Isolation of the vaporiser is still possible, but interlocks between the inlet and outlet valves to prevent total isolation are rarely fitted. This is because it is occasionally necessary to close both valves during cleaning and overhaul. A safe system of work for maintenance and operation is thus a vital part of the safety arrangements, and is a requirement under the PSTGC Regulations.[23]

Pressure control valve

166 All vaporiser designs incorporate an element of superheating of the vapour, either in the vaporiser itself or as a separate unit. This is necessary to prevent chlorine reliquefying in the control valves, where it could cause problems of irregular pressure in operation. These problems are avoided by reducing the gas pressure at the exit from the vaporiser. A suitable pressure-reducing control system is recommended.

Corrosion

167 Corrosion of the vaporiser tubes or coils could lead to a loss-of-containment accident. The consequence of a minor chlorine leak from the chlorine side of a vaporiser heating bath could be very serious since the mixture of chlorine and moisture will lead to rapid corrosion of the evaporator surfaces and a substantial release of chlorine.

168 You must arrange for a competent person to periodically examine your vaporiser and other pressure systems in accordance with your written scheme of examination.[54] A competent person [53] must certify that the written scheme for examination is suitable for the purpose of preventing reasonably foreseeable danger to people from the unintentional release of stored energy from the system. The written scheme of examination should describe the nature and frequency of the examination. This should be based on risk assessment and give due consideration to the duty and the condition of the vaporiser when it was last inspected. The competent person will advise on suitable examination and test regimes, and when the vaporiser should be replaced. Examination intervals between one and five years are typical. Coil-in-bath evaporators are commonly given a rigorous inspection every two years, and the coils are discarded if seriously pitted. Some manufacturers advise that the coils should be renewed every two years. Following examination the equipment should be thoroughly dried to a dew point less than -40°C before recommissioning. Moisture left in the system can lead to very rapid corrosion. The procedure should be covered by a written operating procedure.

169 Corrosion of the heat exchanger surfaces is not directly monitored. Instead the evaporator vessel or tubes are frequently protected against water corrosion by cathodic protection. Typically the anodes should be checked visually every three to six months. The frequency should be established by experience of the rate at which the anodes are consumed and replaced. If the anodes are found wholly consumed at inspection, a thorough examination of the vaporiser should be undertaken. The water bath or condensate outlet should be monitored for chlorine leaks by redox or conductivity measurements. This early warning of minor leaks is helpful in all cases, and is very strongly recommended if cathodic protection is not provided or not maintained.

170 Accumulation of solid deposits reduces the effectiveness of a vaporiser and can also enhance corrosion. The vaporiser needs to be cleaned and dried to a dew point less than -40°C regularly. Close attention to the cleaning procedure will minimise corrosion but typically, the chlorine evaporator cylinder in a hot water bath (see Appendix 7, type 1c system) should be renewed after five years. The old one may be submitted to a competent inspection body for certification for further use if required.

CHLORINE ABSORPTION SYSTEM

171   You should give detailed consideration to ensure that in all chlorine-using operations chlorine can, in an emergency, be vented to an absorber without emission to the environment.

172   Control of chlorine emissions from prescribed processes (see paragraph 10) must be the subject of consultations with the Environment Agency in England and Wales and SEPA in Scotland.

173   In some installations, the nature of the consuming process is such that absorption of the chlorine is possible without a special absorption unit. However, in such circumstances operators need to ensure that during maintenance periods adequate absorption capacity is always kept available to accommodate any chlorine emissions. A separate absorption plant may not be essential in, for example cooling-water treatment plants and bleach liquor production plants.

Lute pipe (baromaetric leg) and vent for absorption system

174   For most bulk storage installations, however, a separate chlorine absorption plant is required and it should always be maintained in a state of readiness. The quantity of reagents available in the absorption system needs to be adequate to deal with any foreseeable emergency. The inlet to the scrubbing system should include a lute pipe (barometric leg) to prevent liquid from the scrubbing system entering the chlorine system.

175   The responsibility for the installation of an adequate chlorine absorption system rests with the consumer, but you should obtain the chlorine supplier's advice on the proposed installation.

176   Consider carefully the provision of adequate instrumentation with alarms and the disposal of effluent from the chlorine absorption plant.

177   Adequate standby equipment should be provided to cover breakdowns and routine overhauls. Essential circulating pumps, fans and instrumentation should be among those items which are connected both to the mains and to the factory emergency power supply if there is one. When the absorption facility is required to be continuously available (eg vents from reactors) it is essential to provide emergency power and stand-by circulating pumps or an emergency gravity-fed supply of absorbing solution.

Vent collection system

178   The pipelines for the collection of the vent gases containing dry chlorine may be made of mild steel but back-diffusion of moisture from the absorption system, which may occur if ventings are intermittent, has to be prevented.

179 Vent systems from relief systems, which are likely to operate only infrequently, may be protected from back-diffusion of moisture by the use of protective membranes. In some cases it may help to provide a controlled dry gas purge through the vent lines.

180 If there is any risk of moisture contamination, the pipework has to be made of rubber-lined or plastic-lined carbon steel, or plastic resistant to wet chlorine (eg PVC, Hetron or Atlac 382), or glass.

181 If there is any possibility of liquid chlorine carry-over, liquid gas separators should be installed on the lines to avoid excess pressure or overloading of the absorption system; these separators are fitted with a temperature alarm to indicate the presence of liquid chlorine in the separator. Furthermore, if it is possible for liquid chlorine carry-over to take place, plastic pipework should not be used. Pipework should be sized to take account of the maximum possible flows under the most unfavourable conditions.

Absorption equipment

182 Various types of absorbers are used for the treatment of vent gases; suitable absorbers may be based on the use of packed towers, vent injectors or sparge absorbers. It can be an advantage if the system selected gives a suction on the plant.

183 Caustic soda liquor is the most convenient reagent for absorption of chlorine in waste gases. The concentration of caustic soda should not exceed 21% NaOH because of the risk of salt deposit causing blockages in the absorption plant. It is recommended that the flow of chlorine is controlled or restricted by an orifice plate to an acceptable maximum, so that the temperature rise in the absorber does not reduce its effectiveness.

184 Alternatively, for installations where there is no bulk storage for caustic soda liquor and where lime or soda ash is available on the site, a lime slurry or a soda ash solution may be used.

Instrumentation

185 It is essential that faults are detected quickly. Adequate instrumentation with alarms should be provided on the vent absorption plant to ensure there is a warning if equipment fails. Significant faults are:

(a) Loss of circulation.

(b) Chemical depletion of the absorbing solution. Depletion of the solution can be monitored by the use of redox or conductivity measurement.

186 Consider providing a pressure indicator fitted with an alarm to show if there is excessive venting or a blockage in the absorption system.

DESIGN AND LOCATION OF INSTALLATIONS

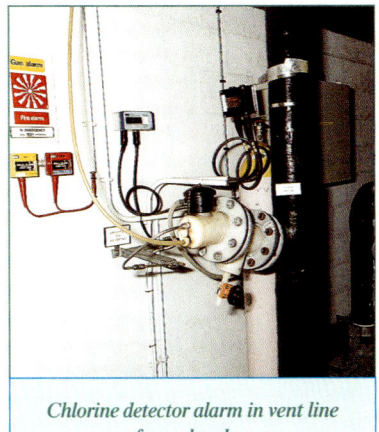

Chlorine detector alarm in vent line from absorber

187 A monitor to detect chlorine should be installed on the outlet from the absorber. On detecting chlorine the following actions are needed:

(a) raise the alarm.

(b) isolate the flow of chlorine to process; and

(c) increase the flow of liquor to the vent scrubber.

The flow from the vent line to the scrubber should be maintained. Isolating the flow to the scrubber may put people at risk.

Disposal of effluent from the chlorine absorption plant

188 The disposal of the liquor from the chlorine absorption plant requires careful consideration, as the presence of hypochlorite may create problems. If the waste liquor is discharged without treatment, the possibility of interaction with other effluents should be investigated (eg a mixture with acid effluent can lead to evolution of chlorine in the effluent mains, and with ammoniacal effluent can lead to formation of nitrogen trichloride).

189 Under some circumstances it may be necessary to treat the effluent to reduce hypochlorite content to an acceptable level before discharging to a sewer. Your chlorine supplier and your local Environmental Health Officer should be consulted on an environmentally acceptable means of disposal. For highly contaminated effluent you should consult the Environment Agency or in Scotland, the Scottish Environmental Protection Agency.

Operating and maintenance procedures, training and PPE

OPERATING INSTRUCTIONS

190   One of the main risks of chlorine escape to the environment is from incorrect operation of the plant. Operating procedures and the selection and training of process operators are therefore extremely important considerations for the efficient and safe operation of chlorine installations. Your operating procedures need to cover each process operation and meet legal requirements eg see references 18, 23, and 55-60 and the standards recommended in industry guides (see Appendix 4 and reference 22).

191   Written instructions are required for:

(a)   plant maintenance (see paragraphs 193-198);
(b)   plant commissioning inspection and testing (see paragraphs 199-209);
(c)   plant modification and shut-down (see paragraphs 210-213);
(d)   all process work and procedures involved in the unloading of liquid chlorine tankers (see paragraphs 214,215);
(e)   operation of the storage installation and utilisation of the chlorine (see paragraphs 214-229); and
(f)   emergency action to deal with chlorine spillages and gas escapes (see paragraphs 247-263).

These may take different forms depending upon the complexity of the installation, eg from simple guide cards for straightforward operations to complete manuals for complex operations and installations.

192   You should make the site manager or other designated person responsible for authorising any amendments to the procedures or schedules. You need to ensure that copies of the instructions include a flowsheet and indicate the valves to be closed in an emergency. Instructions need to be available in the working area for operators, and in the control room or control centre for operators and supervisors. Supervisors should check regularly that operations are carried out precisely according to the written instructions.

MAINTENANCE, INSPECTION AND INSTALLATION

General maintenance requirements

193   Satisfactory maintenance of plant, equipment and instrumentation is essential to minimise risks. The main Regulations that you need to comply with are: COSHH Regulations [20], MHSW Regulations [18], and PSTGC Regulations (regulation 12). [23-25] The CIMAH Regulations [5] (to be replaced in February 1999 by the COMAH Regulations - see Appendix 3), will also apply, depending on the size of the installation and the operating conditions.

194   You will need to prepare maintenance schedules defining the required frequency for servicing, testing and inspection. These schedules should be strictly adhered to. Appropriate records of the results must be kept as required by the PSTGC Regulations 1989 and COSHH Regulations. The need for a written scheme of examination (WSE) [54] is a separate requirement (ie regulations 8 and 9) of the PSTGC Regulations. Other aspects of maintenance are indicated in paragraphs 19, 44, 51, 56-58, 71, 81, 86-89, 98, 127, 136, 143, 160-162, 165, 169, 173, 174, 225, 232, 233, 237, and 255.

195   You need to ensure that detailed written instructions covering all routine maintenance operations are available. These should be formally approved and issued by the responsible maintenance engineer. Supervisors should check regularly that work is carried out according to these procedures. Pay particular attention to corrosion (see also paragraphs 167-170), especially where lagging is used; and to chlorine detector systems to keep such monitoring equipment in effective operation.

196   Close liaison is necessary between the maintenance engineer and the process manager, to ensure that maintenance work is started only after the equipment concerned has been adequately prepared by process personnel and is free from chlorine.

197   Adequate training is required for all maintenance personnel. This should include basic information on the properties of chlorine, safety precautions and emergency procedures (see also paragraphs 231-234).

Maintenance of connections

198   The inspection and replacement procedures for hoses and connections must be documented in accordance with the written scheme of examination. [54] Records of the inspections and replacements should be kept. You need to:

(a)   Carry out engineering inspections of hoses at least once a year, or per every 1000 operations.

(b)   Renew connections at regular intervals, or as required as a consequence of the engineering inspection. Flexible hoses should be renewed on either a fixed time schedule or number of transfers as advised by the hose supplier.

(c)   Hydraulically pressure test replacement flexible connections and dry them with dry air to a dew point less than -40°C before use.

Inspection and commissioning of chlorine tank installations

199 It is your responsibility to organise and control inspections, testing and the commissioning of your storage tank. Your chlorine supplier, as a matter of policy, will give advice if requested to do so and visit the plant before it is commissioned. They deliver chlorine only if they consider your installation to be satisfactory. Your equipment installer also has responsibilities under Section 6 of the Health and Safety at Work etc Act. You and your installer have responsibilities under the PSTGC Regulations; in particular the written scheme of examination (WSE) must be in place before the pressure system goes into service.

200 You should determine the scope of the scheme for the examination of the pressure system, with expert advice being obtained if required. The WSE must specify all inspection and testing techniques employed as required by Regulation 8 of PSTGC Regulations. The WSE report must contain specific details of any deterioration found in the vessel or vessel ancillaries (see Regulations 9 of PSTGC Regulations). It should state which parts of the system have been examined, the condition of those parts and the results of the examination.

201 Initial inspection and testing should be carried out in accordance with the design code (see paragraph 88). The first thorough in-service examination of a vessel specified for liquid chlorine duty should be made by a competent inspecting authority [24] within five years of commissioning and preferably within two or three years. Thereafter the frequency of further thorough examinations should be determined by the inspecting authority and noted in the examination report as required by Regulation 9 of the PSTGC Regulations. The WSE can only be modified after an examination is complete. The examination interval should not normally exceed five years.

202 A competent person [53] to carry out such examination should have the knowledge, experience and resources to search for, detect and assess particular defects associated with systems containing chlorine. Resources should include access to appropriate non-destructive testing and laboratory facilities, together with professional technical ability to relate inspection findings to appraisal of vessel integrity, safe working parameters and future use. The competent person must assess the vessel for continued use with chlorine with respect to:

(a) maximum and minimum safe working pressures;

(b) maximum and minimum safe working temperatures; and

(c) safe working loads at supports and foundations.

Such information should be noted on the examination report, together with the latest date for the next examination.

203 For lagged tanks, you need to remove sufficient lagging to enable the condition of the external surface of the tank to be assessed.

204 Routine hydrostatic testing is not normally recommended. It is, however, recommended if any modifications are made to the storage vessels. Such modifications require a further examination by the competent person.

Inspection procedure

Preparation for internal inspection

205 Before opening the storage vessel for inspection (see also paragraph 168), the vessel needs to be emptied of liquid chlorine and purged to remove all traces of chlorine. Procedures for this should be covered by precise operating instructions [46] and normally include:

(a) breaking of all pipework connections to the vessel by removal of spools or by blanking off;

(b) removing the manlid and filling the vessel with water to which soda ash has been added to neutralise acidic material which forms when water is added to ferric chloride - the contents of the vessel should be stirred thoroughly throughout the process;

(c) siphoning off the water and checking the atmosphere in the vessel for chlorine and oxygen content;

(d) controlling internal inspection of the vessel in accordance with the conditions set out in the Confined Spaces Regulations 1997 [59] and the Code of Practice [60] (see Appendix 3).

Re-assembly after inspection

206 Procedures for this include:

(a) draining off all water;

(b) thoroughly drying the vessel by dry air or nitrogen and removing and replacing joints on all connections to the vessel;

(c) re-fitting the manlid;

(d) pressurisation of the vessel with dry air and measurement of the dew point of the air released;

(e) successive pressurisation with dry air and release until the dew point of the air leaving the vessel is less than -40°C.

207 It is good practice to overhaul all valves on the vessel at the time of inspection. Following overhaul they need to be dried out and stored in individual plastic bags pending reinstallation. Ancillary equipment should also be overhauled at each inspection. Bursting discs should always be renewed.

Testing (See current version of HSE Guidance Note GS 4 Safety in Pressure Testing)[61]

208 Following completion of re-assembly of the equipment and drying out to the required level, you need to:

(a) leak test with dry compressed air or nitrogen at around 8 bar gauge for several hours; then

(b) introduce a small quantity of chlorine to the storage vessel and pressurise with compressed air or nitrogen to around 8 bar gauge;

(c) test all joints for leakage by releasing ammonia vapour from an ammonia bottle and observing the absence of the formation of white fumes of ammonium chloride (this is a very sensitive and well-established method).

If there is no sign of leakage, you should leave the tank under pressure for about a further 12 hours and then repeat the leakage test.

209 All associated pipelines, which need to have been dried out to a dew point less than -40°C, are then gas-tested for leakage. Any leaking joints need to be made gas-tight before introducing liquid chlorine into the system.

MODIFICATION OF THE CHLORINE SYSTEM AND CLEARANCE PROCEDURES

210 You should only modify the chlorine system after conducting a risk assessment (and possibly HAZOP).[50] This ensures that approval is given by responsible staff covering the operating and engineering sections involved, and that appropriate procedures are put in place to deal with any required alterations. Proposed major modifications should preferably be discussed with your chlorine supplier.

211 The Pressure Systems and Transportable Gas Containers Regulations 1989 [23] require (Regulation 4) you to make arrangements for proper control of repairs and modifications to pressure systems. Any modifications or repairs which could affect the integrity of the system have to be defined and overseen by a competent person.

212 Formal clearance procedures need to be established as part of a permit-to-work system [46] for:

(a) ensuring that the plant is in a satisfactory condition for maintenance and internal examination, appropriately isolated and free from chlorine;

(b) covering all work in the chlorine area which requires the use of cranes, mobile equipment, welding sets or other plant which could lead to accidental damage to the chlorine system. This safeguard is necessary even if the work does not directly involve the chlorine-containing lines or equipment;

(c)   formally accepting that the plant is safe for operation after the work has been completed.

213   The storage installation must be emptied of liquid chlorine during inspection and maintenance of the expansion vessel unless provision has been made for alternative means of release of pressure.

UNLOADING OF LIQUID CHLORINE FROM ROAD TANKERS TO STORAGE

214   Transfer of liquid chlorine from tankers to liquid chlorine storage may be achieved either by use of dry compressed air or dry nitrogen or by use of chlorine gas pressure. The methods employing dry compressed air or nitrogen are simpler and the use of chlorine gas pressure is normally encountered only in special circumstances. The gas supply pressure needs to be about 1.7 bar above the pressure in the storage vessel (ie the saturated vapour pressure of chlorine at ambient temperature) to effect the transfer of liquid chlorine from the transport vehicle to storage.

215   You should base your operating procedures for unloading on the outline given in Appendix 6. The procedures should specify requirements for inspection and testing of couplings before use (see paragraph 198). Some operational details are summarised in points (a)-(f):

(a)   Visual inspection, before use, with particular attention to threads. (NB hydrocarbon oils or greases must not be used on threaded or other connections - see Appendix 2, and paragraph 56(j).)

(b)   Use of new gaskets (see paragraph 56(h)) each time connections are made to the tanker. Compressed asbestos fibre (CAF) gaskets are not recommended for environmental reasons. If CAF is used the discarded gaskets should be collected and disposed of safely, bearing in mind that they contain asbestos.

(c)   Proving of the tightness of all connections before introducing liquid chlorine. A gaseous chlorine test is recommended (see paragraph 208c) after a dry air/nitrogen test.

(d)   Capping pipes after use and protecting pipes to reduce the possibility of accidental damage to threads or ingress of moisture, and provide an additional safeguard against an accidental release of chlorine due to an error in valve operation.

(e)   Consider continuous purging with dry air or nitrogen (dew point less than -40ºC).

Testing for leaks with ammonia bottle (see also para 208c). The driver tests the joints near the tanker dome

(f) It is important to vent 'padding gas' to the absorption system (see paragraphs 171-184) after the transfer operation is complete, to restore the pressure in the tank to about the vapour pressure of chlorine at the temperature of the tank contents. If this is not done, the tank may over-pressurise as it warms up, and cause the relief system to operate.

USE OF ISO (DEMOUNTABLE) TANK CONTAINERS

Chlorine ISO tank container on route

ISO tank container: detail of the connection point

216 An ISO tank container is a pressure vessel mounted in a substantial steel frame. They are used predominantly for rail and sea transport and where containers need to be stacked. They vary in capacity, and in the case of chlorine the largest vessels can hold about 14 tonnes. ISO containers are usually sized to meet customer requirements and invariably each tank is designated to a specific customer. If your planned consumption of chlorine is not enough to justify investment in a bulk tank and too great for transportable containers [1] to be used, an ISO container may be appropriate. If the container changeover period exceeds four weeks you should discuss the use of one tonne drums with your proposed supplier.

217 The driver is responsible for ensuring that the ISO container trailer is correctly berthed, the motive unit is uncoupled, and that the landing legs on the corners of the trailer are in place.

218 The design of the ISO berth should be similar to the requirements for an off-loading bay for road tankers (see paragraphs 31-41) eg the ground must be level and the area well-lit, away from traffic etc. The ground surface needs to be resilient enough to prevent the local loads from the landing legs damaging the surface or allowing sinking. Consider spill containment (eg use kerbing, semi-bunding or collection sumps) in the event of any incident. Although the frame provides substantial impact resistance, to prevent damage to the tank and its fittings you should provide crash protection similar to that required for fixed tanks. Similarly, you should provide crash protection for your plant against inadvertent movement during the berthing operation.

219   You will need to provide suitable flexible hose connections to connect the tank to your process. These should be of sufficient length and unobstructed routing so that a leg collapse would not stress the hose or connecting joint.

220   You will also need to draw up procedures for connecting and disconnecting the tank to your process. These procedures and the associated interlocks are effectively the same as for road tanker unloading operations (see paragraphs 35, 39-41, 214, 215 and Appendix 6). They need to be carried out with the motive unit uncoupled and always with the driver present as it is the driver who is responsible for making/breaking and testing the integrity of the joint. Barriers should be lowered when the ISO is berthed and the barrier linked mechanically or by software sequence to the flexible hose connection as drive away protection. As the ISO tanker is not fitted with a relief valve (a regulatory requirement [14]) measures must be taken to prevent overpressure from radiant heat sources such as stored flammables, or from inert gas supplied to raise the pressure in the tanker transferring chlorine to the process.

221   You will need to agree precautions with your supplier to ensure there is no potential for reverse flow from your plant into the ISO tank (see paragraphs 224-229) and implement them.

TRANSFER OF CHLORINE TO THE CONSUMING UNITS

222   Transfer of liquid chlorine from the storage tanks to the consuming units may be achieved by:

(a)   using the vapour pressure of the liquid chlorine alone;

(b)   padding the chlorine storage tank with dry compressed gas;

(c)   transfering the liquid chlorine to a separate tank from which it is pumped using a pump specially designed for use with liquid chlorine.

Methods (a) and (b) are normally the most satisfactory for customer installations.

223   Under exceptional circumstances and by agreement with your chlorine supplier, liquid chlorine from the tankers may be transferred directly to your process or to a chlorine vaporiser. This is a special and unusual arrangement; the adequacy of the control systems and procedures should be verified by a risk assessment. If you see a regular need for this arrangement you should consider the use of ISO tank containers (see paragraphs 216-221).

Transfer of gaseous chlorine

224   With the exception of venting, you should avoid the discharge of gaseous chlorine from tankers or storage vessels directly to a process. Such a procedure can cause a potential hazard [51] by concentrating the trace amounts of the unstable substance, nitrogen trichloride, normally present in the chlorine - see also Appendix 2, paragraphs 15, 20. In addition, a risk of suck-back of moisture or other materials into the vessel or tanker exists (see also paragraphs 100,161).

OPERATING AND MAINTENANCE PROCEDURES, TRAINING AND PPE

Transfer of liquid chlorine using vapour pressure

225   For many applications, the vapour pressure of the liquid chlorine in the storage tank is adequate to transfer the liquid chlorine to the consuming unit, although there may be problems in cold weather with outdoor installations, as the vapour pressure will fall as the liquid chlorine cools. If the demand rate is likely to cause problems in cold weather one of the methods below (paragraphs 226, 227) should be used. When the liquid has been removed from the tank, it may also be acceptable for part of the remaining gas to be used on process. However, a minimum positive pressure should always be maintained in the storage vessels; this should be defined for each system. You should be aware that this method increases the risk of nitrogen trichloride accumulation in the tank and you should implement additional monitoring. [52]

Transfer of liquid chlorine by padding with dry compressed gas

226   Transfer by padding the storage tanks with dry compressed gas is straightforward; the action and precautions which will be required are similar to those detailed in paragraphs 134-141.

Transfer of liquid chlorine using a separate pumping tank

227   Completely enclosed 'canned' pumps have been developed for transfer of liquid chlorine: these are used when the chlorine is required at higher pressure, typically above 7 bar gauge, or when the use of dry inert compressed gas is not acceptable. The liquid chlorine is first transferred from storage to a separate pumping tank which usually consists of a pressure vessel with a bottom connection. The liquid chlorine is withdrawn from the bottom of the pumping tank to the suction of the pump. A remotely operated valve is preferably installed inside the tank or between the pumping tank and the pump for isolation in emergency. The design of this system should ensure that the nett-positive-suction head (NPSH) is adequate to meet the minimum requirements for the pump used. If you see a need for this arrangement you should seek advice from your chlorine supplier at an early stage.

Precautions

228   You should make arrangements to rapidly stop the flow of liquid chlorine from the storage vessel in the event of failure at the chlorine consuming plant (see paragraphs 35, 79, 95-97). Long liquid chlorine pipelines to consuming units may need to be protected against overpressure (see paragraphs 61-67).

229   You need to design the installation to prevent, or minimise the risk of suck-back of aqueous solutions or process liquids from an absorption system. This requires detailed consideration at the design stage and might involve the installation of a non-siphoning barometric leg or a reverse flow/pressure-measuring device.

General guidelines for training

People have legal duties to comply with the safety procedures associated with their work. However, it is never sufficient simply to presume that staff will know and understand what to do. Positive instruction and training is needed. Health and safety training should take place during working hours and should be part of the job.

Training is vital in helping to prevent incidents and to minimise the consequences if they do happen. Think about who should be trained, in what, and to what level of competence.

Training will help employees understand the health and safety aspects of their work. Initial training for new staff should be followed up with new or refresher training as required.

Training must include anyone who works on the site. Operators, managers, staff and occasional visitors, such as maintenance contractors, may all need some training.

Training can take many forms, ranging from on-the-job training linked to information notices, written instructions etc, to formal training courses. The type of training should be appropriate to the activities and duties of those to be trained and the hazards at the site.

Involve and consult staff. Where there is a recognised trade union safety representative, they will need to be consulted. They will know many of the hazards occurring in everyday situations. Cater for unusual occurrences.

Information, instruction and training must be understood by those to whom they are given. If poor performance shows that training is not working, the training will need to be reviewed and improved. Do not assume that previous experience or formal qualifications will mean that new employees do not need training. (You are advised to keep a training record for each staff member, so that it is clear what training they have received and, therefore, which duties they can be expected to perform.)

OPERATING AND MAINTENANCE PROCEDURES, TRAINING AND PPE

230 It is essential that the personnel selected are of adequate physical fitness and they should pass a medical examination before engagement. Operators need to be capable of effective communication and be reliable under stress conditions. Previous experience in the chemical or similar industry is very desirable.

TRAINING

231 You need to ensure that site personnel are properly trained and practised in each procedure. You should develop and implement a training programme which includes both 'off-the-job' and 'on-the-job' aspects. You should regularly assess the programme for its effectiveness.

232 Off-the-job training needs to include basic information on the following:

(a) statutory requirements, ACOPs and guidance;

(b) Physical, chemical, and toxic properties of chlorine;

(c) safety precautions;

(d) personal protective equipment;

(e) process operations and system configurations;

(f) safe systems of work including 'permits-to-work';

(g) container types, methods of handling and security;

(h) operational procedures;

(i) maintenance procedures;

(j) defect rectification;

(k) automatic control systems;

(l) leakage detection systems;

(m) emergency procedures, including leakage containment; and

(n) chlorine suppliers' support facilities.

Maintenance engineers need to be provided with more detailed training on these topics, together with training on system integrity testing, pressure reduction, and safety devices.

233 On-the-job training needs to be carried out under the guidance of an experienced operator/maintenance engineer who is familiar with the process, with

an emphasis on safety precautions and methods of dealing with emergencies. Give particular attention to the following aspects:

(a) the hazards and characteristics of chlorine;

(b) safe methods of plant operation, including connection to and disconnection from supply systems, and regular monitoring and verification of the adequacy of the systems adopted;

(c) methods of maintenance and inspection, in particular the application of relevant standards and codes (see also paragraphs 193-198).

(d) special operations; eg, plant shut-down and start-up, methods of isolation [46] and preparation of equipment for periodic maintenance and inspection;

(e) the location and operation of emergency shut-off valves, ventilation equipment, alarms, leak detectors etc;

(f) the procedures to be followed if a release occurs, these should include isolation and containment of the release and emergency plans; the procedures will need to be site-specific and cover different scales of release (see also paragraphs 247-263);

(g) training in the use of all personal protective equipment (PPE) supplied (see paragraph 237). Maintenance staff should also cover defect rectification.

Competency and audit

234 Competence in the above topics needs to be assessed through post-training assessments using documented procedures. It is recommended that training and safety procedures are audited annually by management or an audit team with relevant experience as part of your company's audit programme. Internal audits may be supplemented by external audits from chlorine suppliers under the CIA's initiative for responsible care and product stewardship, or by other competent people at intervals of approximately three years.

PERSONAL PROTECTIVE EQUIPMENT (PPE)

235 Chlorine is a highly toxic substance; acute exposure can be fatal (see Appendix 1). You therefore need to establish safe working practices and control measures (including PPE) and ensure that they are understood by operatives. Safe procedures are vital where it is necessary to enter an enclosed storage space or a room where a chlorine leak has occurred. Work in such confined spaces is subject to The Confined Spaces Regulations 1997. [59] Guidance on how to comply with the Regulations is given in an Approved Code of Practice. [60] The precautions identified must be implemented and suitable training given to operators.

236 A common source of exposure to chlorine is in operations involving the making and breaking of chlorine pipework connections, particularly to containers. Steps should be taken to

OPERATING AND MAINTENANCE PROCEDURES, TRAINING AND PPE

prevent or, where that is not reasonably practicable, reduce personal exposure to chlorine [20] by means other than personal protective equipment. When PPE, including respiratory protective equipment, needs to be worn, equipment manufactured after 30 June 1995 should carry the 'CE' mark, to indicate that the equipment has been designed and tested to meet the basic requirements of Council Directive 89/686/EEC.

237 Respiratory protective equipment (RPE) that has been approved by the HSE or is claimed by the manufacturer to conform to a standard approved by HSE, and which was manufactured before 1 July 1995, can continue to be used at work, provided that it is still suitable and maintained in good condition. All personnel who are required to use RPE (eg, respirators, breathing apparatus, or escape breathing apparatus) must receive adequate instruction and training in its safe and correct use. The RPE must be thoroughly examined and tested in accordance with the manufacturer's recommendations (typically at least once every month) and records kept.[20]

Selecting suitable respiratory protective equipment (RPE)

238 Where PPE including respiratory protective equipment (RPE) needs to be worn, you must ensure that it is properly selected and that it provides adequate protection. [63, 64] When selecting RPE you should consult relevant guidance [65, 66] and base your selection on the results of a risk assessment. [20] The selected RPE must:

(a) provide adequate protection for your particular circumstances (eg for specific tasks or for emergency escape); and

(b) be compatible with other demands of the job and the working environment.

The selected RPE should make the overall risk of injury while wearing RPE as low as reasonably practicable.

239 When selecting RPE for a particular application, a two-stage selection procedure is therefore recommended:

(a) Based on the results of your exposure risk assessment:

(i) decide whether a respirator or BA, or either may be used; then

(ii) determine the minimum protection required from the RPE. This is done using the equation below. In deciding the maximum allowable concentration inside the facepiece you will need to take account of recognised exposure limits (see Appendix 1) or take account of your in-house limits.

$$\text{Minimum Protection Required} = \frac{\text{Workplace concentration outside the facepiece of the RPE}}{\text{Maximum allowable concentration inside the facepiece of the RPE}}$$

For emergency escape purposes where the exposure will be less than 15 minutes, the maximum allowable concentration in the above expression is the Short-Term Exposure Lmit (STEL) (see Appendix 1). Now compare the Minimum Protection Required value with the Assigned Protection Factors (APF) indicated in HSG53[66] and identify a selection of equipment. (APFs shown in HS(G)53 have been published by the British Standards Institution).[67] These APF figures are a guide, not a hard and fast rule. Indeed, it should be recognised that protection levels below the APF are possible when RPE is *unsuitable* for the task and is *not* suited to the wearer and the environment. Where advice given in HSG53 is properly taken into account, it is possible to achieve protection at or above the published APF values. You may use higher APFs if you have good quality information (eg satisfactory face-fit results for those wearing RPE) to demonstrate that they apply in your workplace conditions and to the selected RPE. You can use the APF for the equipment selected to estimate concentration inside the facepiece.

$$\text{Concentration inside the facepiece} = \frac{\text{Workplace concentration outside the facepiece}}{\text{APF}}$$

Note: *'Nominal Protection Factors' (NPF) values have been used in the past, for identifying a selection of equipment. This procedure is no longer valid because workplace studies have shown that many wearers may not achieve the level of protection indicated by NPFs.*

(b)   The next stage is to take account of the factors detailed in paragraphs 36-47 of HSG53 to help narrow down the choice. Always involve the wearers in the selection process, and where possible provide them with a choice of suitable RPE. This will help to ensure that it is suited to them individually, and increase the chances that it will be accepted and worn correctly.

Where there is doubt about the choice, you need to confirm with the manufacturer or supplier that the chosen equipment is suitable for the task and the conditions in which it is to be used. They have duties under the Health and Safety at Work Act etc 1974 to provide information on the limitations and capabilities of their RPE.

240   At some chlorine installations it is common practice for personnel to carry half mask respirators fitted with suitable filters (eg: type and class: B1; colour: grey) for protection against chlorine. The purpose of this type of respirator is to provide an immediate protection in the event of an incident involving low concentrations of chlorine gas so that the wearer can escape into fresh air. This type of half mask respirator has an APF = 10, ie the maximum allowable workplace concentration = 10 x STEL = 10 ppm.

Driver wearing full face mask fitted with a filter. (Helmet removed for demonstration purposes)

241   A full face mask with cartridge or canister has an APF of 40. The use of this type of respirator would typically be in or very near the open air during the connecting up or disconnecting of containers or breaking into previously purged chlorine systems. The operating procedures specific to the site should state whether the

respirator has to be worn for each operation, or be 'at the ready' to be put on in case of need. A respirator (eg a mask fitted with a filter or canister) is not suitable for use in atmospheres which are immediately dangerous to life or health. In other words, respirators are not suitable for operations where there is a potential for a significant release of chlorine gas. In these circumstances a suitable breathing apparatus (BA) should be worn.

242   Filters have a shelf-life specified by the manufacturers beyond which they should not be used. Once filter-canister seals have been broken, filter life will depend on usage, contaminent concentrations, breathing rate etc. Your risk assessment, combined with information from the filter manufacturer, will determine the useful life of respirator filters; your decisions need to be communicated to the wearers. Once unsealed, filters should not be stored for re-use, but they may be used over a number of consecutive days, provided they have not been exposed to concentrations of chlorine similar to or above those they are provided for.

243   A negative pressure demand BA with full face mask has an APF of 40. For major leaks a positive pressure demand BA with full face mask (ie a self-contained BA) would be appropriate, provided the minimum protection required was consistent with the APF (2000), see paragraph 253. A self-contained breathing apparatus (SCBA) should always be worn (possibly with a gas-tight chemical protective suit) when entering an enclosed space or chlorine room where a significant leak has been detected or suspected. This is because the chlorine detector may be some distance away from the source of the leak or pockets of 'trapped' gas which are not dispersed by the ventilation system. The concentration in such areas may be much higher than those detected by the alarm system.

244   In certain circumstances, compressed airline breathing apparatus (CABA) may be suitable. However, these restrict the movement of the personnel and the trailing hose can add to the risk in areas with obstructions. In such situations a self-contained breathing apparatus may be appropriate.

245   For indoor installations with multi-stage alarms, the forced ventilation system will have been switched off on activation of the higher level alarm. People entering the area to identify and eliminate the source of the leak should wear suitable BA, see paragraphs 252-255). No person should work alone in these circumstances. Any back-up staff in attendance for emergency action should wear suitable BA 'at the ready'.

246   Emergency escape BA is not intended for use during normal work and therefore it is not recommended by HSE for anything other than emergency escape use.

Emergency arrangements

Note: Further guidance will be available when the COMAH Regulations come into force in February 1999.

247 You need to inform the appropriate Fire Authority and Police Force of the presence of chlorine at your site. You should also involve them and your chlorine supplier at an early stage when developing and updating your emergency plan and procedures. Your emergency arrangements should be based on a risk assessment and include procedures on how gas releases may be dealt with safely by site personnel and on whether to call for assistance from beyond the site.[68, 69, 70] Your risk assessment should also address fire safety of the process or installation and possible impacts from neighbouring sites. General fire precautions should comply with the requirements of the Fire Precautions (Workplace) Regulations 1997.[21]

248 Your emergency plan should cover the foreseeable range of chlorine releases for your site; a summary of some of the important elements of a plan is given in Appendix 8. A copy of the plan should be made available to all personnel involved in its implementation. It is recommended that the plan includes the names or positions of the persons who will sound the off-site alarm. This may be someone on-site, or it may under some circumstances be the responsibility of the first Fire Officer on the site in the event of an emergency. The plan should also include first-aid (see Appendix 1) and evacuation arrangements both on-site and, if appropriate, off-site (see Appendix 8).

249 Each installation needs to have means of warning all workers that a gas escape has occurred. A wind direction indicator, mounted in a highly visible location, needs to be provided to help personnel decide the best direction in which to escape. The appropriate action to be taken following a gas escape warning should be defined in written instructions, and appropriate training given.

250 For a minor gas escape, you may only need to plan simple actions. In other circumstances however, a further system of special warnings may be required, which initiates the emergency plan and, if necessary, the off-site emergency plan. The first call for assistance should be to the emergency services for incident control and rescue, and then to Chlor-Aid, through your supplier who will offer advice on

how to deal with the release. Under Chlor Aid the chlorine producers and suppliers (see Appendix 4) collaborate in dealing with chlorine emergencies at bulk installations throughout the UK. The arrangements are outlined in a booklet published by the CIA [71] under the chemical industry's Responsible Care initiative.

251   Arrange regular practices of the emergency plan. Some of these should involve the emergency services, who will advise on a suitable frequency.

EMERGENCY EQUIPMENT

252   Your risk assessment should consider the extent, type, and location of the emergency equipment, including the need for chemical protection suits which provide total encapsulation. These can be compressed airline supplied full suits or full protective suits worn over self-contained breathing apparatus (SCBA).

253   SCBA with full face mask conforming to BSEN 137 (SCBA) [72] or airline BA conforming to BSEN 139 [73] has an APF of 2000 (but see paragraphs 238-246). Self-contained equipment will supply air for up to about 40 minutess (see the manufacturer's details). These sets are provided with a warning system to alert the wearer to leave the contaminated area when the air cylinders are becoming empty. Compressed airline breathing apparatus provides the same protection without a time limit, but does restrict freedom of movement in search and rescue operation.

254   As with other RPE, emergency escape breathing apparatus should be CE-marked and incorporate face protection (eg in the form of a hood or full face mask). Suitable HSE-approved escape equipment may also be used if it was manufactured before 1 July 1995. Such equipment is for escape only and not for use during routine work.

Emergency and rescue equipment

255   Emergency and rescue equipment should be available and readily accessible in all chlorine plant areas, and its location suitably marked. Such equipment needs to be regularly inspected and maintained. An inventory of the equipment should be kept and attached to the plant operational and emergency procedures.

CONTROL OF LEAKAGES

256   Local alarm stations to provide early warning of chlorine escapes are an essential link in the emergency procedure. The use of chlorine detectors and alarms is covered in paragraphs 113-118. Local alarm stations (push-button type preferred) should be located at strategic points near chlorine storage installations; generally two alarm stations on convenient escape routes from the chlorine unloading terminal/ storage tank area are sufficient. The local alarm stations may actuate the works emergency alarm directly or indirectly by raising an alarm in the emergency control centre and the main control room. Preferably in large works the local

EMERGENCY ARRANGEMENTS

alarm station should actuate a distinct local chlorine alarm to warn people off from the affected area.

257   The alarm stations may also actuate the remotely operated shut-off valves on the chlorine storage tanks where this is consistent with the safe operation of the user plant.

258   Materials and equipment including sand and plastic sheets to contain spills of liquid chlorine should be readily available. Covering a stabilised spill with plastic sheets is often the best action. Application of foam would cause renewed evolution of vapour because of the heat supplied. The need for foam and water sprays should be discussed with the chlorine supplier and local fire authority, since the use of foam and water may, in certain circumstances, aggravate the problem. The fire authority may carry stocks of suitable foam, but the decision to use it should be taken in conjunction with the senior technical manager on site.

259   Water should never be added to a spillage of liquid chlorine or sprayed onto a leaking tank. However, water hoses or fog sprays directed at a chlorine gas cloud can help dilute it as a result of the air entrainment generated by the jets of water.

Releases inside buildings

260   If the spill is indoors and contained by the use of sand or a bund it will rapidly cover itself with a coating of slushy chlorine hydrate and a cold vapour layer. Such a stabilised spill should be covered with a plastic sheet (see paragraphs 258 and 259). For a severe leak, possibly arising from a failure of pipework, the chlorine building will provide some delay to the release of the gas to the open air, provided vents and apertures are closed or sealed. This will give more time for the technical staff and management to identify and deal with the source of the release. In dispersing the contained release from a chlorine room it is still essential to consider the off-site consequences and it may be necessary to sound the off-site alarm (when fitted) to alert people to go indoors and remain there. It is for the emergency services to consider clearing people from the area immediately downwind of the installation after such a release.

261   A significant reduction in the release of chlorine from a building is only obtained if the leak is quickly controlled and the rate of air change in the chlorine room is low. The ventilation system should, therefore, be switched off (unless a scrubbing system is installed to remove chlorine from the exhaust gas) and all apertures need to be closed or sealed.

262   Consider using an additional sensor capable of measuring concentrations up to 500 ppm and giving a visual display outside the chlorine room and in the works control room. Such a display is useful for assessing the significance of the leak and whether it can be isolated safely. Once concentrations exceed 1000 ppm (this is

about the threshold concentration for the cloud to be visible), personnel dealing with the release should take additional precautions and should withdraw to a safe area as soon as they are aware that they are breathing contaminated air.

263 After a leak or substantial release has been dealt with it will be necessary to ventilate the chlorine room thoroughly. Operators should not remove any RPE until they have removed clothing (which may be contaminated with chlorine) and are in a safe environment.

Appendix 1
Toxicological properties and first aid

TOXICITY

1   Chlorine has a perceptible odour that can be detected by most people at a concentration of 0.3 ppm (v/v) and by some at concentrations as low as 0.02 ppm. The Occupational Exposure Standard (OES)[74] for exposure to chlorine is 0.5 ppm; this is a time-weighted average concentration over a period of 8 hours. The Short-Term Exposure Limit (STEL)[74] is 1 ppm; a time-weighted average over 15 minutes.

2   It produces clear sensory irritation at concentrations of 0.5-1 ppm and above.[75] Irritation of the mucous membranes of the eye and nose, and especially of the throat and lungs, is caused by exposure to chlorine at levels of around 1-15 ppm. In general, irritation becomes intolerable at concentrations of about 4 ppm.[76] Concentrations of 50 ppm or more are dangerous even for exposures of about 5-10 mins; they may cause inflammation of the lungs with accumulation of fluid. Occasionally the development of respiratory symptoms may be delayed for up to two days after exposure. However, there is no convincing evidence of serious long-term sequelae following recovery from a single exposure to chlorine.[75]

3   Exposure to 1000 ppm may be fatal after a few breaths.[77] Death results from lung damage. It can either occur rapidly (from within hours to a couple of days post-exposure), due to oedema and congestion, or it can be somewhat more delayed (several days) due to secondary pneumonia.

4   The harm from exposure to chlorine is proportional to the 'toxic load' defined as the product of the square of the concentration and exposure time. For risk assessment work, HSE uses a 'dangerous toxic load' [78] (DTL) of: DTL = 108 000 ppm^2min which is potentially fatal to the most vulnerable members of the population. Thus exposures to 104 ppm for 10 minutes or 73 ppm for 20 minutes etc are potentially fatal; the chance of fatality depends on many factors.[78]

FIRST AID

5   When liquid chlorine comes into contact with the skin or mucous membranes it can produce serious burns which need to be treated by a medically competent person. People who have inhaled chlorine gas should be moved as quickly as possible into 'fresh air', laid in a restful position with the head and chest raised, and kept warm. It is essential that qualified medical attention is obtained quickly, as serious symptoms may develop up to 48 hours later. Anyone who has been affected by chlorine gas should be examined locally by a medically competent person or sent to hospital by ambulance.

6   First-aid attendants should be aware of the dangers arising from gassing by chlorine. The following basic rules should be observed:

(a) if chlorine has affected the eyes, they should be irrigated with plenty of clean (preferably tap) water;

(b) contaminated clothing should be removed in a well-ventilated area and affected skin washed with plenty of water;

(c) mouth-to-mouth resuscitation should not be given if the patient is breathing, because there is a risk of the attendant being harmed. However, oxygen may be administered or resuscitation equipment used by suitably qualified personnel.

More comprehensive guidance is given elsewhere.[79]

Appendix 2
Characteristics of chlorine

1   Chlorine is a greenish-yellow gas at ambient temperature and pressure. It is supplied commercially as a liquid under pressure.

2   Commercial liquid chlorine conforms to BS 3947:1976.[80] This Standard specifies a minimum limit for the chlorine content and maximum levels for water content and residue on evaporation; details of the methods of analysis for gaseous impurities (carbon dioxide, oxygen and nitrogen), water content, nitrogen trichloride, and residue on evaporation are also given.

3   Traces of dissolved gaseous impurities in chlorine are not normally significant for most applications; moisture content however is extremely important because of the corrosive nature of wet chlorine.

4   Trace residues which are left on evaporation, usually chlorinated organic products or ferric chloride, may lead to blockage of pipelines, valves or instruments. Nitrogen trichloride can be potentially dangerous[51,52] if the vaporisation process leads to its concentration in residues, but this is generally not considered to be a problem in drum and cylinder installations.

5   *Physical properties*

Atomic weight   35.46

Molecular weight   70.91

Density *liquid*   1561 kg/m^3 at -35°C
                      1468 kg/m^3 at 0°C
                      1410 kg/m^3 at 20°C

        gas   3.173 kg/m^3 at 0°C and 1 bar absolute (relative density 2.490 at 20°C relative to air)

Boiling point at 1.0133 bar absolute   -34.05°C
Melting point   -101.6°C
Critical temperature   144°C
Critical pressure   77.1 bars absolute
Vapour pressure at 20°C   6.7 bars absolute
Viscosity: liquid at 20°C   0.35 cp

1 volume of liquid chlorine = 463 volumes of chlorine gas at 0°C and 1 bar absolute

1 kg of liquid chlorine = 0.319 m^3 of chlorine gas at 0°C and 1 bar absolute

The variation of the vapour pressure of liquid chlorine with temperature is given in Figure A2.1.

Thermal properties

Specific heat (liquid chlorine between 1°C and 27°C) 0.236 kcal/kg/°C

Specific heat (gas at constant pressure at 6.9 bars absolute or less and between 1°C and 27°C) 0.113 kcal/kg/°C

Ratio of specific heat at constant pressure to specific heat at constant volume 1.355

Latent heat of fusion   21.6 kcal/kg

Latent heat of vaporisation at 0°C   63.2 kcal/kg

Coefficient of cubic expansion (liquid chlorine at 20°C) 0.0021 per °C

This coefficient is sufficiently large to result in excessive pressure should liquid chlorine be trapped in pipework between two closed valves with no gas space.

Heat of reaction of chlorine gas with sodium hydroxide liquor 348 kcal/kg of chlorine.

6   While the above data give a general summary of the physical and thermal properties of chlorine, more detailed information is needed for use in plant design calculations.

APPENDIX 2 CHARACTERISTICS OF CHLORINE

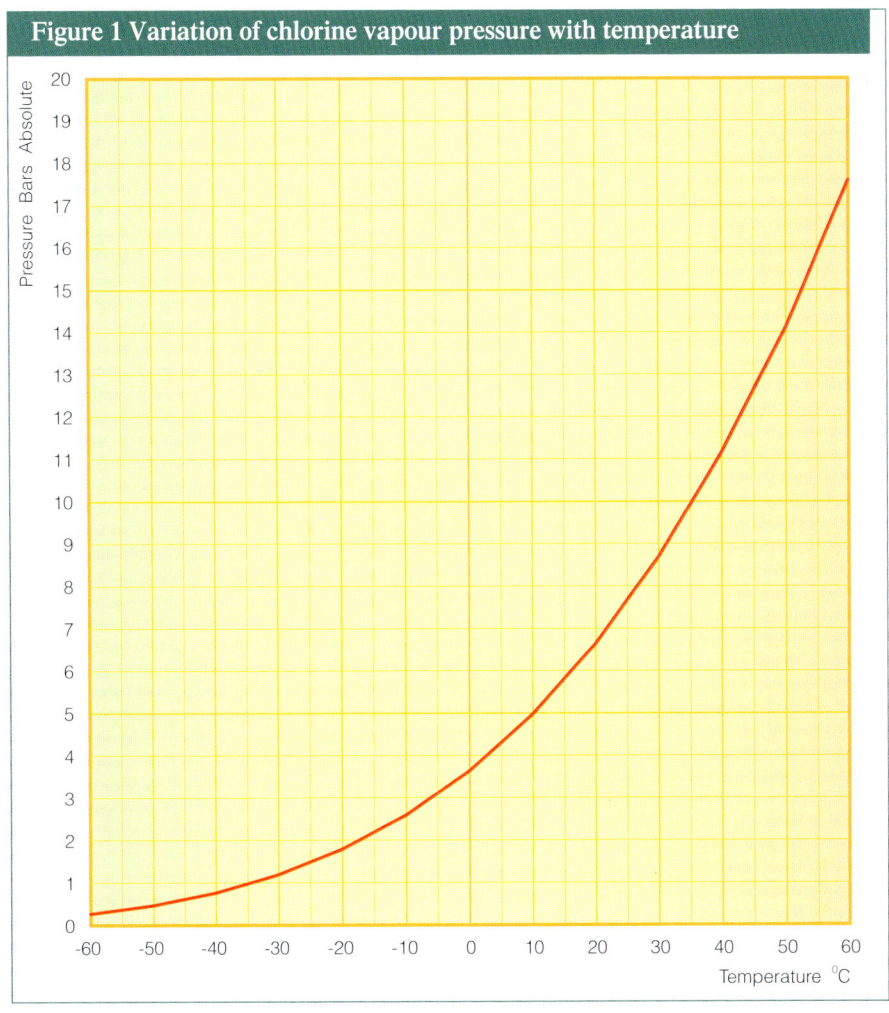

Figure 1 Variation of chlorine vapour pressure with temperature

Solubility of chlorine in water

7 Chlorine dissolves slightly in water to give a solution which has oxidising, bleaching and germicidal properties. The solubility of chlorine in water increases with the partial pressure of the chlorine. The table below gives the solubility of chlorine in water at different temperatures for a total pressure of 1 bar absolute:

Temperature °C	10	15	20	25
grams of chlorine per litre of water	9.97	8.5	7.29	6.41

For a total pressure of 1 bar absolute, the partial pressure of chlorine reduces as the water temperature (and hence the partial pressure of water vapour) increases.

Safety advice for bulk chlorine installations

8   On cooling below 9.6°C, crystals of chlorine hydrate ($Cl_2.8H_2O$) are deposited. For this reason, wet chlorine in process must always be kept above this temperature to avoid the blockages which would otherwise occur as a result of the formation of solid chlorine hydrate.

9   A solution of chlorine in water forms hydrochloric acid and hypochlorous acid:

$$Cl_2 + H_2O \longrightarrow HCl + HOCl$$

Chemical properties

10   Dry chlorine at ambient temperatures reacts directly with many of the elements producing chlorides both of non-metals (eg sulphur or phosphorus) and of metals (eg iron in a finely divided form, aluminium or titanium). Dry chlorine at ambient temperature does not attack steel, copper or nickel, but these metals are attacked at higher temperatures. Steel combines with dry chlorine above 200°C and, since the reaction is exothermic, the rate of reaction may increase rapidly. Reaction with nickel does not take place until the temperature exceeds 500°C.

11   Traces of moisture in chlorine lead to rapid corrosion of steel, copper and nickel.

12   Titanium is resistant to wet chlorine between 15°C and 100°C but reacts violently with dry chlorine and should *not* be used; but see paragraph 18.

13   Chlorine dissolves in cool aqueous solutions of alkalis to produce solutions of hypochlorites; in hot or boiling aqueous alkalis, chlorates can be produced.

14   Chlorine reacts vigorously with many organic compounds including mineral oils and greases, producing chlorinated products. The mechanism is either direct addition to unsaturated bonds or substitution of hydrogen. In the latter case, hydrogen chloride is formed as a by-product.

15   Mixtures of chlorine and hydrogen are explosive over a large range of concentrations; the explosion may be initiated by a spark, by photochemical action or by a catalyst. Under certain conditions chlorine reacts with ammonia to produce nitrogen trichloride, which is spontaneously explosive. This is not a risk when testing for leaks with a bottle of ammonia.

APPENDIX 2 CHARACTERISTICS OF CHLORINE

Selection of materials of construction

16   The choice of appropriate materials of construction for chlorine systems is considered in detail elsewhere.[81] Your options should be selected only after a detailed survey of all possible variations in operating conditions, and your preferred option decided in consultation with your chlorine supplier.

17   A system constructed of steel, which is appropriate for dry chlorine, must itself be dried adequately before commissioning. This may be done by purging with dry air or inert gas until the exit purge has a dew point below -40°C. However, the upper operating temperature must be limited.

18   The use of titanium metal for wet chlorine is satisfactory,[81] provided that the moisture level is always kept high and that control is exercised over the upper and lower operating temperature limit. Maintenance and inspection procedures must include awareness of the possibility of crevice corrosion. However, where titanium is used in plants containing wet chlorine (gas or liquid) consideration should be given to the possibility of a fault condition giving rise to contact between titanium and dry chlorine gas or liquid. If such a fault could possibly arise it may be best to consider alternative construction materials.

19   Materials which are resistant to attack by both wet or dry gaseous chlorine at ambient temperatures include glass, stoneware, porcelain, tantalum, ebonite and certain plastics. The use of plastic materials with *liquid* chlorine is unsatisfactory.

LEARNING FROM INCIDENTS

20   An interesting selection of incidents, which illustrate some of the above hazards (including a nitrogen trichloride explosion, a titanium/chlorine fire and external corrosion) and the means for controlling them, is reviewed in GEST/AP1.[82]

Appendix 3
Relevant legislation and HSE guidance

1   The basis of health and safety law in the UK is the Health and Safety at Work etc Act 1974. This sets out general duties which employers have towards employees and members of the public, and those that employees have to themselves and each other. These duties are qualified in the Act by the principle of 'so far as is reasonably practicable'; ie the extent of the measures taken to avoid or reduce a particular risk to health and safety needs to be balanced against the time, trouble, cost, and physical difficulty involved. This balancing process[83] is often referred to as making risks 'as low as is reasonably practicable' (ALARP).

2   In essence, what health and safety legislation requires is what good management and common sense would lead employers to do anyway: that is to look at what the risks are and take sensible measures to make them ALARP. This broad requirement is made explicit in the Management of Health and Safety at Work Regulations 1992[18,19] (referred to as the Management Regulations). Like the Act, these Regulations apply to every work activity. Other regulations are more specific, eg the Manual Handling Operations Regulations (MHO)[57] or the Control of Substances Hazardous to Health Regulations (COSHH).[20]

3   A full list[3] of current legislation, Approved Codes of Practice and some guidance is published annually. The list contains legislation, which, although in existence, is spent or has lapsed. A price list[84] of all available HSE publications is published annually by HSE Books. Contact details are on the inside of the back cover.

4   A number of regulations (eg COSHH, MHO, PPE,[64] Management Regulations etc) specifically require you to undertake a risk assessment. A leaflet[85] is available describing how these assessments are linked together and what the requirements are; however, it does not deal with highly specialised risks such as major hazards.

5   Under the basic legal requirements you must:

(a) have a written, up-to-date health and safety policy if you employ five or more people;

(b) carry out a risk assessment (and if you employ five or more people, record the main findings and your arrangements for health and safety);

(c) notify occupation of premises to your local inspector if you are a commercial or industrial business;

(d) display a current certificate as required by the Employers' Liability (Compulsory Insurance) Act 1969 if you employ anyone;

(e) display the Health and Safety Law poster for employees or give out the leaflet;[86]

(f) notify certain types of injuries, occupational diseases and events (see paragraph 23); and

(g) consult employees and any appointed union safety representatives[87] on certain issues, such as any changes which might affect health and safety and any information, instruction and training which has to be provided.

6   The ALARP principle and the need for risk assessment enables the Health and Safety Commission, where appropriate, to make Regulations in a goal-setting form: ie setting out what must be achieved, but not how it must be done. Sometimes it is necessary to prescribe in detail what must be done and set absolute standards.

7   Some activities or substances are so inherently hazardous that they require additional arrangements. For example, chlorine installations which store 10 tonnes or more need to meet the general requirements of the CIMAH Regulations (see paragraph 9).

THE NOTIFICATION OF INSTALLATIONS HANDLING HAZARDOUS SUBSTANCES (NIHHS) REGULATIONS 1982 [4]

8   These Regulations implement a notification scheme for installations with inventories greater or equal to specified quantities (10 tonnes for chlorine). Notification is to the Health and Safety Executive via your Local Area Office (see Appendix 4). Under NIHHS the following requirements apply:

(a) before chlorine is used or stored at a site, at least three months notice must be given to HSE and certain details specified;

(b) the notification must be updated whenever there is a change in activity on site or there is an increase or reduction in the operational quantity of chlorine on site; and

(c) the amount of chlorine on site must not be increased to three or more times the quantity originally notified, unless a new notification is made. (Any increases in inventory levels must of course comply with other legislation, in particular section 3 of the HSW Act, ie that the risks to people off-site are ALARP).

THE CONTROL OF INDUSTRIAL MAJOR ACCIDENT HAZARDS (CIMAH) REGULATIONS 1984 [5]

9   These Regulations implement the requirements of the European Directive (82/501/EEC) on the major hazards of certain industrial activities commonly referred to as the 'Seveso' Directive. They apply to the storage and processing of hazardous substances. The Regulations have been amended a number of times.[3] These include the 1988 amendment (revision of threshold quantities for certain substances) and the 1990 modification of the controls on storage following a serious warehouse fire. Two levels of activity are defined. The lower level requirements require companies to take the precautions that are necessary to prevent a major accident and to limit the consequences, and generally to demonstrate safe operation (regulation 4), and to report any major accident (regulation 5). Installations in which chlorine is involved in a process under Schedule 4 are subject to these general requirements regardless of the quantity present, unless the operation is incapable of producing a major accident hazard. Larger (ie top-tier) installations which store 75 or more tonnes, or installations with 25 tonnes or more which carry out process activities under Schedule 4, additionally require the preparation of safety reports, emergency plans and the provision of information to the public (regulations 7-13). Guidance on the CIMAH Regulations is available.[69,88] These Regulations will be withdrawn when the proposed Control of Major Accident Hazards (COMAH) Regulations are implemented in February 1999.

THE COMAH REGULATIONS

10 These Regulations will implement the requirements of The Control of Major Accident Hazards Involving Dangerous Substances Directive (96/82/EC) which was adopted by the EU on 9 December 1996. The Directive is referred to as the 'Seveso II' Directive. The Regulations follow the Directive closely and mirror the Seveso I/CIMAH regime, in having two levels of duties:

(a) general duties on all operators subject to the Regulations: to notify the competent authorities of their activities, to take all measures necessary for the prevention and mitigation of major accidents, to prepare a major accident prevention policy, and report major accidents;

(b) top-tier duties on operators of sites where the quantities of dangerous substances exceed the higher thresholds. These operators must, in addition to the duties in the above paragraph, submit safety reports, prepare and test emergency plans and provide information to the public.

In the case of chlorine the threshold quantities are 10 tonnes for the general duties and 25 tonnes for the top-tier duties. Application depends solely on the presence or anticipated presence of the threshold quantities of dangerous substances, including dangerous substances which might be generated in the course of an accident due to loss of control of an industrial chemical process, with no differentiation between storage and processing. The general duty for operators to take 'all measures necessary for the prevention and mitigation of major accidents' is similar to the CIMAH Regulations which require manufacturers to 'take adequate steps to prevent ... major accidents ... and limit their consequences ...'. In judging how this duty should be complied with in practice, the competent authorities will base their view on whether risks have been reduced to ALARP. The main new requirements are:

- All operators within the scope of the Directive must produce a major-accident prevention policy (MAPP) and ensure that it is properly implemented to guarantee a high level of protection for humans and the environment by appropriate means, structures, and management systems.

- Land-use planning is brought within the scope of the Directive.

- Safety reports (top-tier sites only) have to be made available to the public, but companies can request that certain information, including commercial and personal confidential information, is withheld.

APPENDIX 3 RELEVANT LEGISLATION AND HSE GUIDANCE

- The competent authorities, HSE and the Environmental Agency (EA) in England and Wales, and HSE and the Scottish Environmental Protection Agency (SEPA) in Scotland, must prohibit operations where the measures taken by operators to prevent and mitigate major accidents are seriously deficient.

The Seveso II requirements place much more emphasis on the management of safety and the role of the safety report than in the original Seveso Directive (implemented by the CIMAH Regulations). Paragraphs 11-23 summarise the main requirements of other legislation that is relevant to the control of risks posed by installations handling chlorine.

THE PLANNING (HAZARDOUS SUBSTANCES) ACT 1990 AND PLANNING (HAZARDOUS SUBSTANCES) REGULATIONS 1992 [7]

11 The Act and Regulations introduce planning controls which are designed to ensure that hazardous substances can be kept or used in significant amounts only after the responsible authorities have had the opportunity to assess the degree of risk to people in the surrounding area and are satisfied that the risks are tolerable. In essence the Act and Regulations require sites to apply for 'hazardous substances consent' for inventory levels at or above specific amounts known as the 'controlled quantity' - 10 tonnes in the case of chlorine. Neighbouring sites within 500 m, and controlled by the same person, must be taken into account when deciding the maximum inventory. New sites must obtain hazardous substances consent at an early stage in the life cycle.

12 In England and Wales the controls are enforced by the Hazardous Substances Authority (HSA), usually the District or London Borough Council for the land in question, ie the Local Planning Authority (LPA). In Scotland the equivalent regulations are The Town and Country Planning (Hazardous Substances) (Scotland) Regulations 1993. They are enforced by the Scottish Office, Environment Department (SOED). HSE is a statutory consultee under the Act and advises HSAs and SOED on the nature and severity of the residual risk. The Act recognises that safety must be an overriding control. The controls apply, regardless of whether planning permission is required under other legislation.

13 Guidance on applying for hazardous substances consent in England and Wales is given in *Hazardous Substances Consent: Guidance for Industry* (produced by the Department of the Environment and the Welsh Office, 92 PLAN0001). SOED has issued circular 16/1993 *Hazardous Substances Consent: Guidance for Industry*.

THE DANGEROUS SUBSTANCES (NOTIFICATION AND MARKING OF SITES) REGULATIONS 1990 [39,40]

14 Where more than 25 tonnes of dangerous substances are present on a site (including chlorine) notification must be made to the fire authority and appropriate signs placed at site access points. The enforcing authority is the fire authority except in specified circumstances when it is HSE. The Regulations require all signs to conform to BS5378[41] and to be kept clean and free from obstructions.

THE MANAGEMENT OF HEALTH AND SAFETY AT WORK REGULATIONS 1992 [18]

15 These Regulations implement Council Directives 89/391/EEC (OJ No L183, 29.6.89, p1) and 91/383/EEC (OJ No L206, 29.7.91, p19) on the introduction of measures to encourage improvements in safety and health of workers at work. Under the Regulations you must:

(a) assess the risks to the health and safety of your employees and non-employees arising in, or from, your activities and review the assessment when there is significant change. Records of significant findings of the assessment must be kept where there are five or more employees;

(b) plan, organise, control, monitor and review the preventative and protective measures taken as a result of the assessment;

(c) appoint any competent person(s) needed to help you comply with legal obligations, for example, when having pressure systems examined;

(d) set out what should be done in case of serious and imminent danger at your premises, such as the spillage of an appreciable amount of chlorine;

(e) tell employees about the risks and precautions involved in their work; and

(f) provide health surveillance where necessary.

THE LIFTING PLANT AND EQUIPMENT (RECORDS OF TEST AND EXAMINATIONS ETC) REGULATIONS 1992[89,90]

16 You must:

(a) have certificates of test and examination (normally provided by manufacturers and suppliers) specifying safe working loads before first using chains, ropes and lifting tackle;

APPENDIX 3 RELEVANT LEGISLATION AND HSE GUIDANCE

(b) have chains, ropes, lifting tackle, hoists and lifts thoroughly examined every six months by a competent person (often employed by an insurance company) and obtain and keep the report;

(c) ensure tests and thorough examinations of cranes are carried out before they are first used and obtain a certificate of test and examination specifying safe working loads. Periodic thorough examinations at least every 12 months are also required, for which a report should be obtained and kept.

HSE guidance is available.[90]

Note: These Regulations will be revoked and replaced in December 1998 by the Lifting Operations and Lifting Equipment (LOLER) Regulations (SI 1998/2307). Guidance will be published in an Approved Code of Practice on Safe Use of Lifting Equipment. The Provision and Use of Work Equipment Regulations 1998 (see paragraph 19) also apply to lifting equipment.

THE MANUAL HANDLING OPERATIONS REGULATIONS 1992 [57]

17 These Regulations implement the substantive provisions of Council Directive 90/269/EEC (OJ No L156, 21.6.90, p9) on the health and safety requirements for the manual handling of loads where there is a risk of back injury to workers. Employers must:

(a) avoid the need for hazardous manual lifting and handling if reasonably practicable;

(b) assess the risk of injury from any hazardous manual lifting and handling which cannot be avoided; and

(c) reduce the risk of injury accordingly.

Employees must:

(a) follow safe systems of work laid down by their employers;

(b) use mechanical aids provided by their employers properly; and

(c) remember to use the training provided on lifting.

THE CONTROL OF SUBSTANCES HAZARDOUS TO HEALTH REGULATIONS 1994 [20]

18 These regulations re-enact, with minor modifications, the COSHH Regulations 1988 (SI 1988/1657). They impose requirements on employers using substances hazardous to health to protect employees and other people who may be exposed to such substances. They also impose certain duties on employees concerning their own protection from exposure.

Employers must:

(a) assess risks to health;

(b) prevent exposure;

(c) where prevention is not reasonably practicable, control exposure by, for example, isolating or enclosing the process or, if this is not reasonably practicable, local exhaust ventilation;

(d) maintain control measures in efficient working order and ensure that a thorough test and examination of engineering controls are carried out at suitable intervals. Records of such maintenance must be kept for at least five years;

(e) where prevention or control is insufficient on its own, provide personal protective equipment and maintain it;

(f) inform, instruct and train employees; and

(g) carry out air monitoring and health surveillance where necessary.

THE PROVISION AND USE OF WORK EQUIPMENT REGULATIONS (PUWER) 1992 [55,56]

19 These Regulations impose health and safety requirements with respect to the provision and use of work equipment (machinery, appliances, tools etc). They impose requirements upon employers, including the need to:

(a) provide work equipment that is suitable for the purpose for which it is used or supplied;

APPENDIX 3 RELEVANT LEGISLATION AND HSE GUIDANCE

(b) take steps to ensure that the equipment is not used under conditions for which it is not suitable;

(c) maintain work equipment in an efficient working order and good repair and that any maintenance log is kept up to date;

(d) provide people who use work equipment with:

   (i) clear health and safety information and, where appropriate, written instructions; and

   (ii) adequate training, including the risks involved and the precautions to be taken. (This also applies to supervisors and managers of such people.)

(e) protect people from dangerous parts of machinery by suitable protection devices;

(f) provide suitable and sufficient lighting at any place where a person uses work equipment;

(g) ensure that work equipment is marked in a clear and visible manner with appropriate health and safety information and warnings; and

(h) ensure that any warning device is unambiguous and easily perceived and understood.

Note: These Regulations will be revoked and re-enacted in December 1998. The new PUWER Regulations (SI 1998/2306) include new provisions for mobile work equipment.

THE CONFINED SPACES REGULATIONS 1997 [59,60]

20   These Regulations apply when it is necessary for workers to carry out work in a confined space including a chamber, tank, flue or a similar space, which, by virtue of its enclosed nature, gives rise to a 'foreseeable specified risk'. In the case of chlorine installations the most likely foreseeable specified risk is 'the loss of consciousness or asphyxiation of any person at work arising from gas, fume vapour or the lack of oxygen'. The Regulations prohibit the entry into a confined space for the purpose of carrying out work where it is reasonably practicable to carry out the work by other means. In other situations (for example, the isolation of a leak in a chlorine room) they impose requirements on employers including the need to:

(a) establish safe systems of work for entry to, or carrying out work in, or leaving a confined space that renders the activities safe and without risks to health;

(b) establish suitable and sufficient arrangements for the rescue of people in the confined space in the event of an emergency;

(c) ensure compliance, so far as is reasonably practicable, with the provisions of the Regulations in respect of any work carried out by employees, or other people - in which case the matters need to be within the employer's control.

THE PRESSURE SYSTEM AND TRANSPORTABLE GAS CONTAINERS REGULATIONS 1989 [23,24,25]

21   These Regulations impose requirements for pressure systems containing a gas or liquefied gas at a pressure greater than 0.5 bar above atmospheric pressure. They impose requirements on designers, suppliers of pressure systems and on employers of people who modify or repair such systems. The intention of the Regulations is to prevent the risk of serious injury from stored energy as a result of the failure of a pressure system or part of it. A measure of the stored energy is given by multiplying the system pressure (bar gauge) and volume (litres). A pressure system is:

(a) a system comprising one or more pressure vessels of rigid construction, any associated pipework and protective devices (systems with a stored energy of 250 bar litre or less are exempt from some requirements, eg the written scheme of examination);

(b) the pipework with its protective devices to which a transportable gas container is, or is intended to be, connected; or

(c) a pipeline and its protective devices.

The transportable gas container is not part of the system. Employers must ensure that:

(a) all plant and systems are designed, constructed and installed to prevent danger;

(b) systems are properly maintained;

(c) modifications or repairs do not cause danger;

(d) there is a written scheme for examination[54] of certain pressure vessels, such as chlorine vaporisers, fittings and pipework, drawn up by a competent person;

APPENDIX 3 RELEVANT LEGISLATION AND HSE GUIDANCE

(e) examinations as set out in the written scheme are carried out by a competent person; and

(f) records are kept.

Note: The transportable gas container (TGC) part of these Regulations was revoked in 1996 and incorporated into The Carriage of Dangerous Goods (Classification, Packaging and Labelling) and Use of Transportable Pressure Receptacles Regulations 1996. These PSTGC Regulations will be replaced in November 1999 by The Pressure Equipment Regulations and The Pressure Systems Safety Regulations.

THE PERSONAL PROTECTIVE EQUIPMENT AT WORK REGULATIONS 1992 [63,64]

22 These Regulations impose health and safety requirements when providing PPE and using it to protect people in the workplace. Employers must:

(a) provide suitable PPE free of charge to protect employees against risks which have not been controlled by other means;

(b) take all reasonable steps to ensure it is properly used;

(c) before providing PPE, assess risks to health and safety which have not been avoided by other means and define the characteristics required by PPE to make the risks ALARP; then select suitable PPE by matching those characteristics with those of PPE available;

(d) maintain the PPE provided in clean and efficient working order and provide suitable storage for it when not in use; and

(e) give information, instruction and training.

Employees must:

(a) use PPE provided; and

(b) report any loss or obvious defect to the employer.

THE REPORTING OF INJURIES, DISEASES AND DANGEROUS OCCURRENCES REGULATIONS (RIDDOR) 1995 [91,92,93]

23   These apply to all employers and self-employed people and cover everyone at work. The main points are that you must:

(a) notify your inspector immediately, normally by telephone, if anybody dies, receives a major injury or is seriously affected by, for example, an electric shock or poisoning;

(b) notify your inspector immediately if there is a dangerous occurrence, eg a fire or explosion, which stops work for more than 24 hours;

(c) confirm telephone notifications in writing within ten days on F2508;

(d) report within seven days (on form F2508) injuries which keep an employee off work or unable to do their normal job for more than three days;

(e) report certain diseases suffered by workers on form F2508A; and

(f) keep details of reported incidents.

ENFORCING THE LAW

24   Health and safety laws relating to your firm will usually be enforced by a health and safety inspector from HSE. In some cases, eg a public swimming pool, health and safety law is enforced by the local authority.

25   Inspectors may visit workplaces without notice but you are entitled to see their identification before they come in. They may want to investigate an accident or complaint, or inspect safety, health and welfare at your premises. They have the right to talk to employees and safety representatives, take photographs and samples, and even in certain cases to impound dangerous equipment. They are entitled to co-operation and answers to questions.

26   Inspectors will be aware of the main risks in handling chlorine and will give you help and advice on how to comply with the law. If there is a problem, they may issue a formal notice requiring improvements or, where serious danger exists, one which prohibits the use of a process or equipment. Inspectors have powers to prosecute a firm (or an individual) for breaking health and safety law.

Appendix 4
Useful contacts and standards

CHLORINE PRODUCERS AND SUPPLIERS

Hays Process Chemicals Sandbach, Cheshire CW11 3PZ

Imperial Chemical Industries plc, Chlor Chemicals PO Box 13, The Heath, Runcorn, Cheshire WA7 4QF

Rhodia Ltd Staveley, Chesterfield S43 2PB

The Associated Octel Co Ltd PO Box 17, Ellesmere Port, Wirral, Cheshire L65 4HF

BOC Ltd Special Gases 24 Deer Park Road, London SW19 3UF
(Note: BOC supplies only cylinders.)

Air Products (GB) Ltd Speciality Gases Department, Weston Road, Crewe CW1 1DF
(Note: Air Products supplies only drums and cylinders.)

OTHER USEFUL CONTACTS

Chemical Industries Association (CIA) Kings Buildings, Smith Square, London SW1P 3JJ Tel: 0171 834 3399

The CIA runs a chlorine committee dealing with technical and liaison issues.

Water Services Association of England and Wales 1 Queen Anne's Gate, London SW1H 9BT Tel: 0171 957 4567; Fax: 0171 957 4666

HSE

You can find details of your local HSE office in your local telephone directory or the current edition of HSE35 *The Health and Safety Executive: Working with employers,* available from HSE Books.

You can find details of HSE Books and HSE's enquiry service on the inside back cover of this booklet.

Chlorine Institute Inc. 2001 L Street, NW, Washington DC 20036 USA

Euro Chlor Avenue E Van Nieuwenhuyse 4, Box 2, B-1160 Brussels, Belgium
Tel: +32 2 676 72 11; Fax: +32 2 676 72 41

Euro Chlor publishes a wide range of relevant reports.[22] The new series (AP) of pamphlets on *learning from accidents* is essential reading (eg see reference 82).

UK suppliers of Euro Chlor approved globe valves

Descote Ltd 19 Sandy Lane, Weston Point, Runcorn, Cheshire WA7 4EX
Tel: 01928 565666; Fax: 01928 565646

Shaw, Son & Greenhalgh Ltd Albert Street, Lockwood, Huddersfield HD1 3QG
Tel: 01484 532425; Fax: 01484 512426

British Standards Institute

BSI Sales and Customer Services, 389 Chiswick High Road, London W4 4AL
Tel: 0181 996 7000; Fax: 0181 996 7001

British Standards are available from the above address.

Standards relevant to chlorine

Specification for pipe threads for tubes and fittings where pressure-tight joints are made on the threads (metric dimensions) BS 21:1985

Specification for liquid chlorine BS 3947:1976 (1997)

Specification for filling ratios and developed pressures for liquefiable and permanent gases BS 5355:1976

APPENDIX 4 USEFUL CONTACTS AND STANDARDS

Specification for unfired fusion welded pressure vessels BS 5500:1997

Specification for flat products made of steels for pressure purposes BS EN 10028: Parts 1, 2, 3:1993 and 4:1995

Specification for tolerances on dimensions, shape and mass for hot rolled steel plates 3 mm thick or above BS EN 10029:1991

Circular flanges for pipes, valves and fittings. Part 3: Section 3.1 Specification for steel flanges. Part 3 Section 3.3 Specification for copper alloy and composite flanges BS 1560: Part 3: 1989

Specification for bolting for flanges and pressure containing purposes BS 4882: 1990

Specification for compressed asbestos fibre jointing BS 1832:1991 (1997)

Specification for bursting discs and bursting disc devices BS 2915: 1990

Transportable gas containers. Part 1 Specification for seamless steel gas containers above 0.5 litre water capacity BS 5045: Part 1 1982; *Part 2 Specification for steel containers of 0.5 L up to 450 L water capacity with welded seams* BS 5045: Part 2 1989

Specification for filling ratios and developed pressures for liquefiable and permanent gases BS 5355: 1976

Safety signs and colours. Part 1 Specification for colour and design BS 5378: Part 1 1980 (1995); *Part 3 Specification for additional signs to those given in BS 5378: Part 1* BS 5378: Part 3 1982 (1995)

Polytetrafluoroethylene (PFTE) materials and products. Specification for fabricated unfilled polytetrafluoroethylene products BS 6564: Part 2 1991 (1996)

Specification for identification of pipelines and services BS 1710: 1984 (1991)

Schedule of paint colours for building purposes BS 4800: 1989 (1994)

Guide to implementing an effective respiratory protective device programme BS 4275: 1997

Specification for respiratory protective devices: self-contained open-circuit compressed air breathing apparatus BS EN 137: 1993

Respiratory protective devices: compressed airline breathing apparatus for use with a full face mask, half mask, or mouthpiece assembly. Requirements, testing, marking BS EN 139: 1995

Steels for pressure purposes. Part 3 Specification for corrosion and heat-resisting steels: plates, sheet and strip BS 1501: Part 3 1990

Specification for steels for fired and unfired pressure vessels: sections and bars BS 1502: 1982 (1990)

Appendix 5
Outside installations and inside installations

1 Bulk chlorine installations should preferably be located in the open air. Sometimes it may be appropriate to locate the installation in a building.

2 The building may enclose the entire installation or part of it, eg the manlids, valves, associated pipework, gauges and other equipment, leaving the tank itself outside.

3 The advantages, disadvantages and consequent requirements for outside or inside installations are listed in paragraphs 4-8.

OUTSIDE INSTALLATIONS

4 The advantages of outside installations are that:

(a) leakages are not confined, so the source of leakage is more safely accessible from upwind;

(b) it is easier to identify the point of leakage and take immediate local corrective action;

(c) access for installation and for major maintenance is simpler; and

(d) building costs are lower.

5 The disadvantages of outside installations are that:

(a) leakages may be detected at an early stage only from downwind positions;

(b) small leakages, particularly those arising from corrosion, can develop unnoticed;

(c) maintenance and repair work may have to be carried out in adverse weather conditions;

(d) there is no containment to reduce the rate of release to the atmosphere;

(e) surface corrosion is more likely; any leak may rapidly escalate; and

(f) there is less security.

6   It follows that outdoor installations require:

(a) strict vigilance and protection against corrosion;

(b) protection against possible mechanical damage and unauthorised access;

(c) an appropriate emergency system, possibly including procedures for the use of water sprays for gas clouds (see also main text paragraphs 247-263);

(d) weather protection for maintenance in critical areas; this could be either a permanent canopy or temporary sheeting; and

(e) continuous staffing on the site if a chlorine release could present serious consequences on or off site.

INSIDE INSTALLATIONS

7   The advantages of inside installations are that:

(a) valves and other equipment are protected from rain and snow, and provided the building is kept dry, there will be less risk of corrosion;

(b) background heating is possible, to help provide dry surroundings and increased chlorine vapour pressure for processes where inert gas/air padding is not acceptable;

(c) controlled ventilation is possible, limiting the external effects if the leak is fairly small;

(d) there is greater likelihood of a monitoring device detecting a leak; this is a particular advantage on an unattended plant; and

APPENDIX 5 OUTSIDE INSTALLATIONS AND INSIDE INSTALLATIONS

(e) the installation is protected from accidental mechanical damage, explosion or fire in adjacent plant or interference by unauthorised persons.

8   The disadvantages of inside installations are that:

(a) following a medium or major leak, emergency access may have to be made to a closed room with a high chlorine concentration;

(b) the point of leakage may be difficult to identify, owing to lack of dispersion, and mist formation;

(c) if the building is heated, there will be greater ground evaporation and flash from a liquid leak; and

(d) access for maintenance is likely to be more difficult.

9   It follows that indoor installations require:

(a) adequate forced ventilation systems, including start-up from operating points outside as well as inside the building; and

(b) careful consideration of plant layout and provision of adequate escape routes and escape respiratory equipment.

Appendix 6
Procedures for discharging road tankers of chlorine

Note: *This typical procedure assumes that the storage tanks and associated items of equipment have a safe working pressure of at least 12 bar gauge. If this is not the case, then steps will need to be taken (eg adjust the air system pressure, and relief valve settings) to ensure that the safe working limits for the storage vessels and delivery system are not exceeded. It is important that more detailed and site-specific procedures are developed and agreed by the customer, haulier and chlorine supplier.*

Action by	Action needed
Joint	1 The procedures need to be designed to minimise potential leaks by ensuring that all newly made joints are tested by gas pressure with, at most, only a small amount of liquid. During these test operations a gas mask must be worn. Similarly, a suitable gas mask (see paragraphs 235-246) must be worn during the disconnecting operation when there is a possibility of the escape of a small quantity of residual vapour. During the rest of the operations it should be kept readily available.
Customer	2 Will operate all valves on the bulk storage installation, including the filling pipe.
Driver	3 On arrival at the works, will weigh off on the site weighbridge and proceed to the discharge berth.
Driver	4 Will position the tanker at the discharge berth and employ the drive-away protection. A variety of techniques may be used, eg interlocks to the tanker brakes, wheel chocks, and the removal of the vehicle ignition key to a controlled location. These are in addition (see paragraph 7 below) to any drive-away protection barriers and any interlocks to shut down the discharge should movement of the vehicle or should chlorine be detected (see main text, paragraphs 39-41).

Driver	5	Presents the delivery notes to a responsible official.

In signing these notes the customer accepts the responsibility that there is sufficient space available in the storage tank to receive the full load from the road tank and that the installation is fit and ready for the discharge to proceed.

Driver 6 Will tell the *plant operator* the weight of chlorine in the tanker so that the operator can determine where the final reading will be on the weighing machine dial or load cell indicator.

Customer 7 Will ensure that any warning notices are displayed and barriers are erected, and will operate any safety interlocks associated with the road vehicle berth.

Customer 8 Where there are two or more tanks *the customer* will determine which tank is to receive and check that the storage tank cannot be overfilled. The pressure on the tank before starting the discharge should not normally be greater than 5.9 bar gauge but in very hot weather it may be higher.

Customer 9 The customer will ensure *before* discharge that the vent valve on the stock tank filling pipe is *closed*. When fitted, the barrier mechanical interlock key is used to activate the control panel sequence for the discharging operation and release the off-loading arm.

Driver 10 Establish the vehicle movement detection interlock and activate interlocks to the chlorine detection system before operating valves on the tanker and installation. Wearing a gas mask, remove both caps from the road tank valves and the customer's filling arms and test for leaks. Using new PTFE, aramid fibre or other suitable material for joint rings (preferably not CAF, see paragraph 56), connect both air supply and liquid discharge arms to the appropriate valves on the tanker.

Joint 11 Wearing a gas mask, apply pressure to the discharge connection, preferably by briefly opening the valve to the stock tank. An alternative but less desirable method is to open the tanker discharge valve *momentarily*. The driver (wearing a gas mask) tests the joints on the discharge pipe using ammonia water. If satisfactory, the driver can remove his gas mask and then request the plant operator to open the valve on the stock filling line after the drop arm. The liquid valve on the

APPENDIX 6 PROCEDURES FOR DISCHARGING ROAD TANKERS OF CHLORINE

tanker can be *slowly opened* to fill the delivery line: the pressure observed will be the pressure on the road tanker. Alternatively, and only when the driver is satisfied with the integrity of the connections, the instrument air connections are made which will allow the discharge valves to be operated. This may also activate a brake interlock which is integral with the customer's shutdown system.

Joint   12 Start the air compressor and when the line pressure is 8.3 bar gauge open it to the road tanker. When the road tanker pressure (as indicated on the filling pipe to the stock tank) is 1.7 bar gauge above that of the stock tank request the *plant operator* to open the valve to the appropriate stock tank and commence discharge of the road tanker.

Joint   13 Observe the discharge of the road tanker is proceeding satisfactorily by reference to the weighing machine dial or load cell indicator.

Joint   14 Observe the stock tank pressure as the discharge is proceeding. Should this rises to 6.2 bar gauge the driver requests the customer to crack open the vent valve on the tank to reduce the pressure.

Joint   15 Indication that the road tanker has been completely discharged is:

(a) fluctuation of pressure gauge on the liquid chlorine delivery line;

(b) equalisation of tanker and line pressure readings.

Joint   16 The plant operator closes the storage tank inlet valve and the padding air supply valve. Vent excess pressure from the tanker via the vent valve to the scrubber. The driver then closes the padding air inlet to the tanker and the liquid chlorine outlet from the tanker, and disconnects the operating air leads to them so the tanker valves cannot be reopened. The connecting pipe for padding air can now be vented and disconnected and the tanker padding air connection capped. The operator cracks open the vent valve on the liquid chlorine delivery line to the stock tank filling pipe. When the pressure gauge on the liquid

	chlorine delivery line shows zero (and any hoar frost on the vent valve has begun to disappear) the operator closes the valve on the chlorine delivery line at the tanker discharge point. Close the delivery line vent valve.
Customer	17 Crack open the vent valve on the stock tank for about one minute in order to check that the level of liquid chlorine in the tank is below the bottom of the vent dip pipe (no frosting should appear). This operation also vents non-condensable gases. Check that the pressure in the tank is reasonable for the temperature of the chlorine. The storage is now isolated from the discharge line to the scrubber and the delivery line is purged by pressurising and depressurising (open vent valve and close it when pressure gauge shows zero) with dry air for a minimum of five cycles. The operator can now shut down the air compressor if it is not needed for other operations.
Driver	18 Wearing a gas mask, disconnect the liquid discharge pipe from the tanker, replace the sealing plug to prevent the entry of moist air, and swivel back to the staging. Tell the *plant operator* that the vent can be closed. The short connecting pipes from the liquid and air valves can be disconnected, both valves capped and the tanker dome securely fastened. The RPE can now be removed.
Customer	19 *Under no circumstances allow any section of the pipeline to be left unvented with liquid chlorine trapped between closed valves.*
Driver	20 Before leaving the storage plant ask the designated responsible person to sign the advice note and consignment note after the words 'all operations connected with the discharge of the road tank have been completed satisfactorily'. Hand one copy to the responsible person. On leaving the works weigh again on the site weighbridge.

Appendix 7
Types of vaporiser

Chlorine vaporisers may be divided into four basic types:

(a) Vertical tube bundle.
(b) Coiled tube immersed in a heating bath.
(c) Concentric tube.
(d) Kettle-type evaporator.

VERTICAL TUBE BUNDLE (TYPE 1)

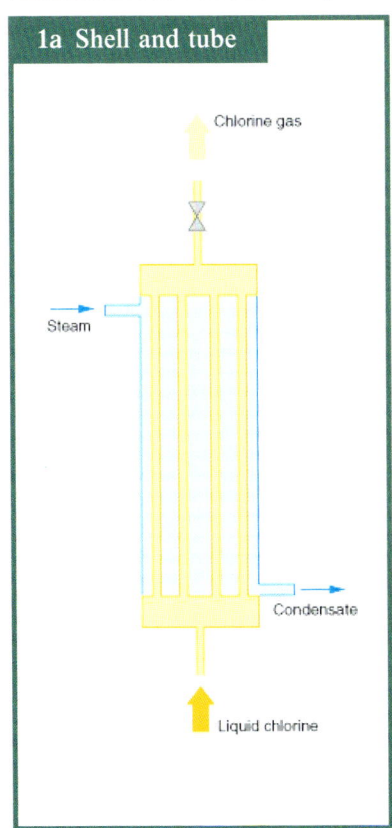

1a Shell and tube

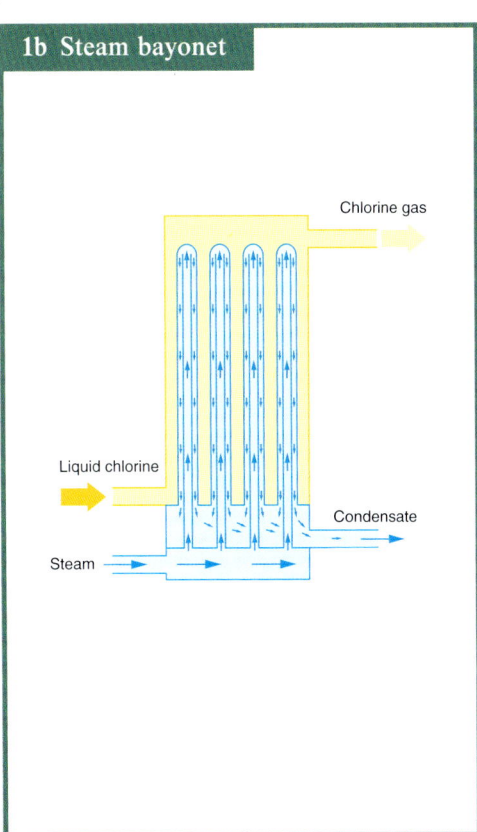

1b Steam bayonet

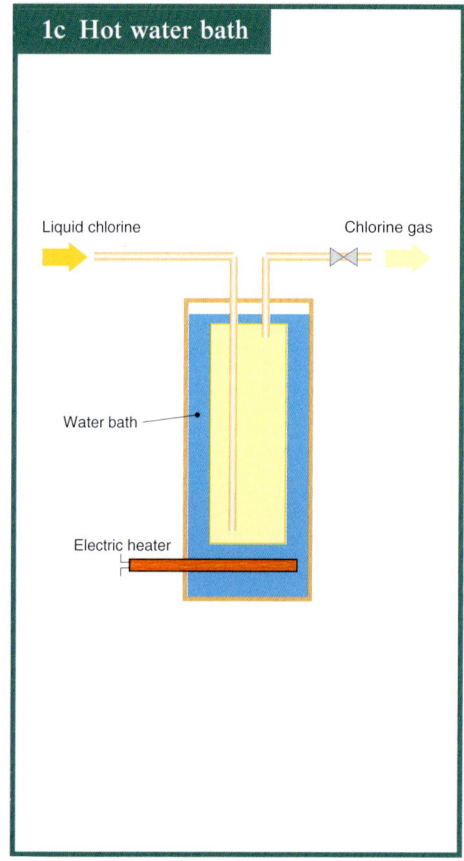

1c Hot water bath

Advantages of this type of system are:

(a) small overall size for relatively large heat transfer surfaces;

(b) easy maintenance; and

(c) for the mode of operation in which the chlorine is in tubes, the liquid chlorine is automatically displaced by over-pressure when the vapour supply to the consuming plant is shut off.

Disadvantages of this type of system are:

(a) for the mode of operation in which the chlorine is in the tubes, there is a risk of instability at high throughput owing to variation of liquid levels and a possibility of corrosion in the region of the liquid surface; and

(b) for the mode of operation in which the chlorine is in the shell, it is difficult to dry out the shell.

COILED TUBE IMMERSED IN A HEATING BATH (TYPE 2)

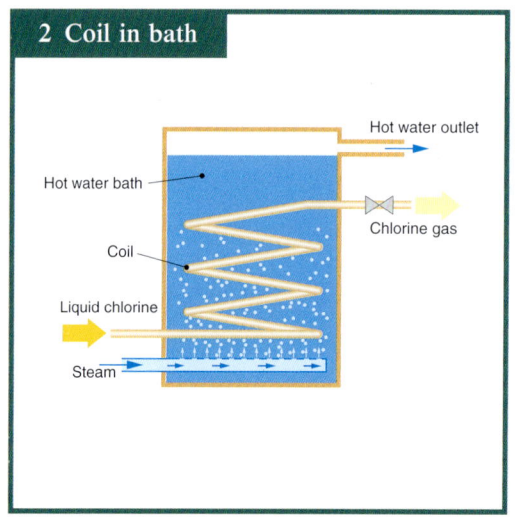

2 Coil in bath

Advantages of this type of vaporiser are:

(a) it is simple to maintain and operate;

(b) the long coil generally ensures adequate superheating;

(c) there are no problems with differential thermal expansion;

(d) plug flow operation avoids concentration of high boiling impurities;

(e) drying out of equipment before use is relatively easy; and

(f) liquid chlorine is automatically displaced when the vapour supply to the consuming plant is shut off.

Disadvantages of this type of vaporiser are:

(a) low throughput;

(b) external corrosion of the tube can easily occur, especially near the liquid surface;

(c) irregular internal erosion of the coil may occur; and

(d) internal inspection and cleaning of the coil is difficult.

CONCENTRIC TUBE UNITS (TYPE 3)

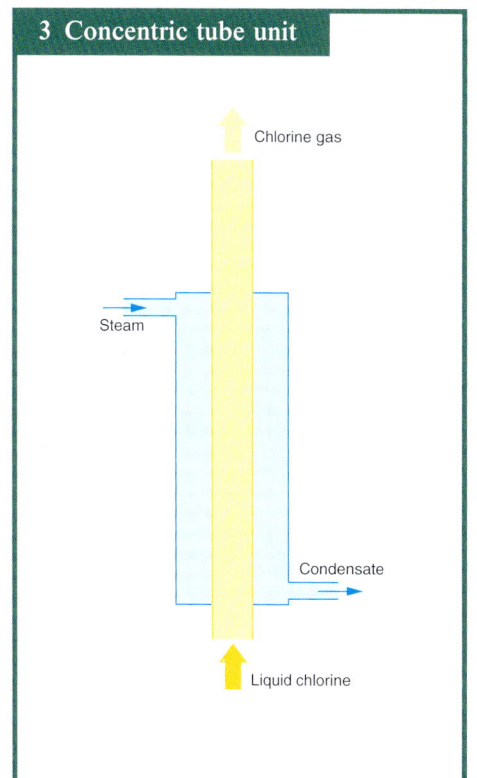

Advantages of this type of system are:

(a) simple construction with minimum welding requirements;

(b) easy maintenance and operation;

(c) easy provision of adequate corrosion allowance;

(d) automatic displacement of liquid chlorine when the vapour supply to the consuming plant is shut off; and

(e) plug-flow operation above a certain minimum flow avoids concentration of high boiling impurities.

Disadvantages of this type of system are:

(a) potential instability of operation at high and low throughput;

(b) limitation of unit capacity owing to relatively small heat transfer surface area; and

(c) greater difficulty in obtaining adequate superheating of the chlorine.

KETTLE-TYPE EVAPORATOR (TYPE 4)

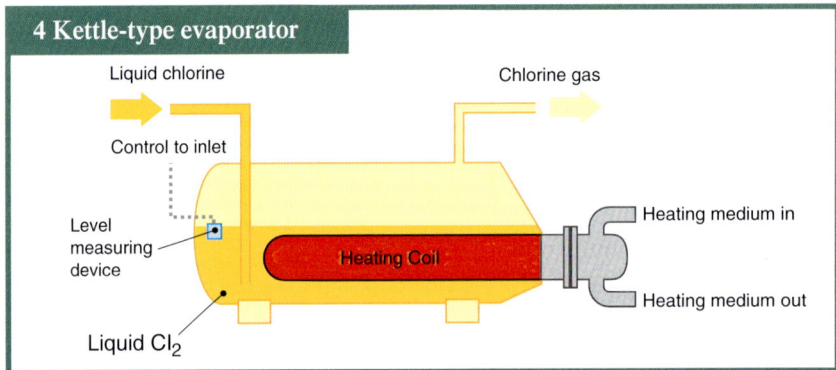

Advantages of this type of system are:

(a) it can be designed for large throughput;

(b) allowance for thermal expansion can easily be made; and

(c) operation is stable, provided that either the level of chlorine in the kettle or the pressure of chlorine fed to the vaporiser, is controlled.

Disadvantages of this type of system are:

(a) since the vessel contains a relatively large amount of liquid chlorine, leakage or excess pressure in the vessel pose a greater potential hazard;

(b) a relief system with a large capacity is required, unless the vaporiser is designed for high pressure;

(c) operation can result in concentration of nitrogen trichloride; the purging process required to reduce this hazard may be difficult to carry out on consumer premises;

(d) drying of the equipment on the chlorine side is difficult; and

(e) dismantling of the tubes is difficult and requires a large space.

Appendix 8
Emergency plans

(**Note:** *A fuller discussion of emergency plans appears in HSE's HSG25[69] and references 17, 70 and 71. Additional guidance will be issued to support the COMAH Regulations.*)

1   The works should have an on-site emergency plan for dealing with a major chlorine release. The plan should include instructions for the emergency team and for non-essential personnel, and for liaison with the emergency services. The emergency plan should be based on paragraphs 247-263. Your plan will depend on the results of your risk assessment and the need to comply with health and safety legislation, eg section 3 of the HSW Act.[2] The following paragraphs contain some elements of a plan.

2   The plan may include detailed instructions for:

(a) raising the alarm;

(b) investigating and assessing the source and extent of the chlorine release;

(c) alerting all personnel on-site or in neighbouring premises and the emergency services; setting up emergency control centres, assessment by key personnel of the incident and consequent emergency measures on and off-site;

(d) methods for controlling the chlorine release;

(e) search systems for casualties, and accounting for personnel on-site;

(f) methods for assessing the directional spread and concentration of the gas cloud;

(g) criteria for determining whether to evacuate non-essential personnel or to advise them to stay inside buildings with doors, windows and ventilation shut;

(h) methods for assessing whether corresponding actions are advisable for people off-site and, in particular, liaison with the manager at any adjacent underground workings where chlorine could enter the ventilation system; advice to emergency services on the direction, spread and concentration of the gas cloud; and

(i) first aid to on-site casualties, and arrangements for evacuation where advisable and practicable; advice to ambulance service on routes to use.

3   Since each installation will have its own special features, a detailed plan relating to the particular plant will be required. Local management should be responsible for preparation of the plan which should be developed in co-operation with the local authority, the police, fire, hospital and ambulance services, and the chlorine supplier. Specific duties are laid on some of these people by the Control of Industrial Major Accident Hazards Regulations 1984. These will be superseded by the requirements of the COMAH Regulations in 1999.

EMERGENCY CONTROL CENTRES

4   Basic requirements for a satisfactory system to deal with an emergency resulting from a serious escape of chlorine are outlined as follows:

(a) two control centres should be provided so that, in the event of a gas escape, operations can be controlled from the centre which is least affected under prevailing atmospheric conditions;

(b) each centre should be provided with a separate external telephone line, as well as with connections to the factory's external and internal telephone system;

(c) adequate emergency equipment (self-contained breathing apparatus, supplies of suitable foam as agreed with the emergency services, protective clothing, etc) should be available (see section on emergency equipment);

(d) emergency first-aid facilities, including equipment for administering oxygen, need to be provided;

(e) a large-scale map (1:25 000 or 1:10 000) of the surrounding area should be available to help determine which parts of the factory and the local neighbourhood are likely to be affected;

(f) wind direction indicators have to be visible from, or indicated in, each control centre; and

(g) equipment and information are needed to assess the likely extent of the gas cloud for various sizes of release and various weather conditions.

5   The emergency plan should specify in advance the individuals and deputies responsible for the action necessary to deal with the emergency.

SITE EMERGENCY TEAM

6   There should be a trained emergency team with the following key personnel:

(a) *Site incident controller* - the senior person on-site responsible for the direction of on-site operations;

(b) *Site main controller* - normally the works manager or deputy with overall responsibility for the operation of the emergency plan, maintaining close liaison with the police and fire services, and for advising them on the risk; and

(c) *Other key personnel* - including:

   (i) the team responsible for the control of the chlorine release;

   (ii) the team responsible for the search for casualties, for first aid and for the control of evacuation.

7   The police will be responsible for dealing with members of the public who might be affected by the chlorine escape; they will need to be advised of the size and expected duration of the release together with the areas which could be affected, to allow the police and the site main controller to agree whether the public should remain indoors or be evacuated.

EMERGENCY ASSEMBLY AREAS

8   Emergency assembly areas should be designated for use in a chlorine emergency by personnel not involved in the emergency team. The assembly areas allow for counting of personnel and for controlled evacuation if the need should arise. Preferably, the assembly area should be at the periphery of the works site with good exit for evacuation. A building with upper storeys at a location upwind of the chlorine release may offer sufficient protection while the release is brought under control. Evacuation of personnel to the assembly areas should be directed

by a senior member of the emergency team who will take wind direction into account. There will be occasions when evacuating off-site is not the best action, for example, when the release is sudden and of limited duration.

CASUALTIES

9   First-aid treatment for casualties is discussed in Appendix 1.

References

1 *Safe handling of chlorine from drums and cylinders* HSG40 HSE Books 1999 ISBN 0 7176 1646 0

2 *Health and Safety at Work etc Act 1974*

3 *List of current health and safety legislation* 1996 HSE Books 1997 ISBN 0 7176 1311 9

4 *The Notification of Installations Handling Hazardous Substances Regulations 1982* SI 1982/1357 HMSO

5 *The Control of Industrial Major Accident Hazards Regulations 1984* SI 1984/1902 HMSO

6 *Council Directive 96/82/EC Control of major-accident hazards involving dangerous substances* Official J of the EC No L10/40 CEC January 1997

7 *The Planning (Hazardous Substances) Regulations 1992* SI 1992/0656 HMSO

8 *Risk criteria for land-use planning in the vicinity of major industrial hazards* HSE Books 1989 ISBN 0 11 885491 7

9 *Environmental Protection (Prescribed Processes and Substances) Regulations 1991* SI 1991/0472 HMSO

10 Environmental Protection Act 1990

11 Alkali and Works Regulation Act 1906

12 *Health and Safety (Emissions into the Atmosphere) Regulations 1983* SI 1983/0943 HMSO

13 *The Carriage of Dangerous Goods (Classification, Packaging and Labelling) and Use of Transportable Pressure Receptacles Regulations 1996* SI 1996/2092 HMSO

14 *The Carriage of Dangerous Goods by Road Regulations 1996* SI 1996/2095 HMSO

15 *Are you involved in the carriage of dangerous goods by road or rail?* INDG234 HSE free leaflet *1996*

16 *Successful health and safety management* HSG65 HSE Books 1997 ISBN 0 7176 1276 7

17 *Formula for health and safety: guidance for small to medium-sized firms in the chemical manufacturing industry* HSG166 HSE Books 1996 ISBN 0 7176 0996 0

18 *The Management of Health and Safety at Work Regulations 1992* SI 1992 /2051 HMSO

19 *Management of health and safety at work. Approved Code of Practice. Management of Health and Safety at Work Regulations 1992* L21 HSE Books 1992 ISBN 0 7176 0412 8

20 *The Control of Substances Hazardous to Health Regulations 1994* SI 1994 /3246 HMSO

21 *The Fire Precautions (Workplace) Regulations 1997* SI 1997 /1840 TSO

22 *Publications: Literature and technical documentation* Euro Chlor 1997*

23 *The Pressure Systems and Transportable Gas Containers Regulations 1989* SI 1989/2169 HMSO

24 *Safety of pressure systems. Pressure systems and Transportable Gas Containers Regulations 1989. Approved code of practice* COP 37 HSE Books 1990 ISBN 0 11 885514 X

25 *A guide to the Pressure Systems and Transportable Gas Containers Regulations 1989* HSR30 HSE Books 1990 ISBN 0 7176 0489 6

26 *The Carriage of Dangerous Goods by road (Driver Training) Regulations 1996* SI 1996/2094 HMSO

27 *The Carriage of Dangerous Goods by Rail Regulations 1996* SI 1996/2089 HMSO

28 *Specification for pipe threads for tubes and fittings where pressure-tight joints are made on the threads (metric dimensions)* BS 21: 1985

29 GEST 75/45 *Flexible Monel hoses for the transfer of gaseous or liquid chlorine* 5th Ed May 1996 Euro Chlor*

30 GEST 75/43 *Flexible steel coils for the transfer of gaseous or liquid chlorine* 7th Ed May 1996 Euro Chlor.

31 GEST 75/44 *Articulated arms for the transfer of gaseous or liquid chlorine* 9th Ed May 1996 Euro Chlor*

32 *Process piping* B31.3 American Society of Mechanical Engineers 1996

33 *Chemical plant and petroleum refinery piping* Supplement to B31.3 American Society of Mechanical Engineers 1995

34 *Specification for bolting for flanges and pressure containing purposes* BS 4882: 1990

35 *Circular flanges for pipes, valves and fittings.* Part 3 Steel, cast iron and copper alloy flanges BS 1560: Part 3 Sections 1-3: 1989

36 *Pipe flanges and flanged fittings* B16-5 NPS 1-2 through NPS 24 American Society of Mechanical Engineers 1988

37 *Specification for compressed asbestos fibre jointing* BS 1832: 1991 (1997)

38 *Polytetrafluoroethylene (PFTE) materials and products Part 2 Specification for fabricated unfilled polytetrafluoroethylene products* BS 6564: Part 2 1991 (1996)

39 *The Dangerous Substances (Notification and Marking of Sites) Regulations 1990* SI 1990/0304 HMSO

40 *Notification and marking of sites. The Dangerous Substances (Notification and Marking of Sites) Regulations 1990. Guidance on Regulations* HSR29 HSE Books 1990 ISBN 0 11 885435 6

41 *Safety signs and colours. Part 1 Specification for colour and design* BS 5378: Part 1: 1980/(1995); *Part 3. Specification for additional signs to those given in BS 5378 Part 1* BS 5378: Part 3 1982 (1995)

42 *Specification for identification of pipelines and services* BS 1710: 1984 (1991)

43 *Schedule of paint colours for building purposes* BS 4800: 1989 (1994)

44 *The Health and Safety (Safety Signs and Signals) Regulations 1996* SI 1996/0341 HMSO

45 *Safety signs and signals. The Health and Safety (Safety Signs and Signals) Regulations 1996. Guidance on Regulations* L64 HSE Books 1997 ISBN 0 7176 0870 0

46 HSC Oil Industry Advisory Committee *The safe isolation of plant and equipment* HSE Books 1997 ISBN 0 7176 0871 9

47 *Specification for filling ratios and developed pressures for liquefiable and permanent gases* BS 5355: 1976

48 *Specification for unfired fusion welded pressure vessels* BS 5500: 1997

49 *Specification for bursting discs and bursting disc devices* BS 2915: 1990

50 Kletz TA *Hazop and Hazan: Identifying and assessing process industry hazards* 3rd ed IChemE 1992 ISBN 0 85295 285 6

51 GEST 76/55 Maximum levels of nitrogen trichloride in liquid chlorine 1990 Euro Chlor*

52 Safe handling of chlorine containing nitrogen trichloride Chlorine Institute Pamphlet 152**

53 *Introducing competent persons. Pressure Systems and Transportable Gas Containers Regulations 1989* INDS29 HSE free leaflet 1990

54 *Written schemes of examination. Pressure Systems and Transportable Gas Containers Regulations 1989* INDG178 HSE free leaflet 1994

55 *Provision and Use of Work Equipment Regulations 1992* SI 1992/2932 HMSO

56 *Work equipment. Provision and Use of Work Equipment Regulations 1992 Guidance on Regulations* L22 HSE Books 1992 ISBN 0 7176 0414 4

57 *The Manual Handling Operations Regulations 1992* SI 1992/2793 HMSO

58 *Manual handling. Manual Handling Operations Regulations 1992. Guidance on Regulations* L23 HSE Books 1992 ISBN 0 7176 0411 X

59 *The Confined Spaces Regulations 1997* SI 1997/1713 TSO

REFERENCES

60 *Safe work in confined spaces. Confined Spaces Regulations 1997. Approved Code of Practice and Guidance* L101 HSE Books 1997 ISBN 0 7176 1405 0

61 *Safety in pressure testing* GS4(rev) HSE Books 1992 ISBN 0 7176 0811 5

62 *Permit-to-work systems* INDG98(rev3) HSE free leaflet 1998

63 *The Personal Protective Equipment at Work Regulations 1992* SI 1992/2966 HMSO

64 *Personal protective equipment at work: Personal Protective Equipment at Work Regulations 1992. Guidance on regulations* L25 HSE Books 1992 ISBN 0 7176 0415 2

65 GEST 92/171 Personal protective equipment for use with chlorine 1995 Euro Chlor*

66 *The selection, use and maintenance of respiratory protective equipment: A practical guide* HSG53 1998 HSE Books ISBN 0 7176 1537 5

67 *Guide to implementing an effective respiratory protective device programme* BS 4275: 1997

68 *Prepared for emergency* INDG246 HSE free leaflet 1997

69 *Control of Industrial Major Hazards Regulations 1984 (CIMAH): Further guidance on emergency plans* HSG25 1985 HSE Books ISBN 0 11 883831 8

70 Robinson BW and UK Chlorine Producers *General guidance on emergency planning within the CIMAH Regulations for chlorine installations* 1986†

71 *Inter-company collaboration for chlorine emergencies* CIA 1992 ISBN 0 900 623†

72 *Specification for respiratory protective devices: self-contained open-circuit compressed air breathing apparatus* BS EN 137:1993

73 *Respiratory protective devices. Compressed airline breathing apparatus for use with a full face mask, half mask or mouthpiece assembly. Requirements, testing, marking* BS EN 139: 1995

74 *Occupational exposure limits* EH40/98 HSE Books (updated annually) ISBN 0 7176 1474 3

75 WHO International Programme on Chemical Safety *Environmental Health Criteria 21 Chlorine and hydrogen chloride* World Health Organisation, Geneva, 1982

76 *Summary criteria for occupational exposure limits* EH64 HSE Books (updated annually) ISBN 0 7176 1576 6

77 Lewis RJ *Sax's dangerous properties of industrial materials* (9th ed) Van Nostrand Rheinhold 1996 ISBN 0 4420 2025 2

78 Turner RM and Fairhurst S *Toxicology of substances in relation to major hazards: Chlorine* HSE Books 1990 ISBN 0 11 885528 X

79 GEST 89/145 Guidelines for medical management of chlorine exposure (3rd ed) 1995 Euro Chlor*

80 *Specification for liquid chlorine* BS 3947: 1976 (1997)

81 GEST 79/82 Choice of materials of construction for use in contact with chlorine (7th ed) Euro Chlor 1995*

82 GEST/AP1 Learning from accidents 1996. Euro Chlor*

83 *The setting of safety standards: A report by the interdepartmental group and external advisors 1996* HM Treasury††

84 *Price list* HSE Books (published annually)

85 *A guide to risk assessment requirements: Common provisions in health and safety law* INDG218 HSE free leaflet 1996

86 *Health and Safety Law. What you should know* (poster) HSE Books IBSN 0 7176 1380 1

87 *The Health and Safety (Consultation with Employees) Regulations 1996* SI 1996/1513 TSO

88 *A guide to the Control of Industrial Major Accident Hazards Regulations 1984* HSR21 (rev) HSE Books 1990 ISBN 0 11 885579 4

REFERENCES

89 *The Lifting Plant and Equipment (Records of Test and Examination etc) Regulations 1992* SI 1992 /0195 HMSO

90 *A guide to the Lifting Plant and Equipment (Records of Test and Examination etc) Regulations 1992* L20 HSE Books 1992 ISBN 0 7176 0488 8

91 *The Reporting of Injuries, Diseases and Dangerous Occurrences Regulations 1995* SI 1995/3163 HMSO

92 *A guide to the Reporting of Injuries, Diseases and Dangerous Occurrences Regulations 1995* L73 HSE Books 1996 ISBN 0 7176 1012 8

93 *Everyone's guide to RIDDOR* HSE31 HSE free leaflet 1996

The future availability and accuracy of the references listed in this publication cannot be guaranteed. Current Regulations, guidance and ACOPs, and current HSE publications are listed in the latest version of references 3 and 84 respectively.

*   Available from Euro Chlor, see address in Appendix 4.
**   Available from CIA, see address in Appendix 4.
†   Available from CIA or chlorine producers, see addresses in Appendix 4.
††   Available from The Public Enquiry Unit, HM Treasury, Parliament Street, London SW1P 3AG Tel: 0171 270 4558

For details on how to obtain HSE priced and free publications, see inside back cover.

List of acronyms and abbreviations

ACOP	Approved Code of Practice
ALARP	As Low As Reasonably Practicable
ANSI	American National Standards Institute
APF	Assigned Protection Factor
ASME	American Society of Mechanical Engineering
BA	Breathing Apparatus
BS	British Standard
CABA	Compressed Airline Breathing Apparatus
CAF	Compressed Asbestos Fibre
CEC	Commission of the European Communities
CIA	Chemical Industries Association
CIMAH	Control of Industrial Major Accident Hazards (Regulations)
COMAH	Control of Major Accident Hazards (Regulations)
COSHH	Control of Substances Hazardous to Health (Regulations)
DTL	Dangerous Toxic Load
EA	Environment Agency
EEC	European Economic Community
EU	European Union
HAZOP	Hazard and Operability
HMSO	Her Majesty's Stationery Office
HSA	Hazardous Substances Authority
HSE	Health and Safety Executive
HSR	Health and Safety Regulations (Booklet)
HSW	Health and Safety at Work
ISO	International Standards Organisation
LOLER	Lifting Operations and Lifting Equipment Regulations

LPA	Local Planning Authority
MHO	Manual Handling Operations (Regulations)
MHSW	Management of Health and Safety at Work (Regulations)
NIHHS	Notification of Installations Handling Hazardous Substances (Regulations)
OEL	Occupational Exposure Limit
OES	Occupational Exposure Standard
OJ	Official Journal (of the European Communities)
PPE	Personal Protective Equipment
ppm	Parts per million (by volume)
PSTGC	Pressure Systems and Transportable Gas Containers (Regulations)
PTFE	Polytetrafluoroethylene
PUWER	Provision and Use of Work Equipment Regulations
RIDDOR	Reporting of Injuries, Diseases and Dangerous Occurrence (Regulations)
RPE	Respiratory Protective Equipment
SCBA	Self Contained Breathing Apparatus
SEPA	Scottish Environmental Protection Agency
SI	Statutory Instrument
SOED	Scottish Office, Environment Department
STEL	Short-Term Exposure Limit
TGC	Transportable Gas Container
TSO	The Stationery Office
UK	United Kingdom
UPVC	Unplasticised Polyvinyl Chloride
WSE	Written Scheme of Examination